A Girl from Hometown,
WEST VIRGINIA

Essays and Poems

Barbara A. Whittington

Special thanks to Elizabeth Vollstadt, friend, author and editor, who's been on all my writing journeys.

All rights reserved. No part of this book may be copied, scanned, or electronically transmitted without the express permission of the author.

Copyright @ 2020 by BARBARA A. Whittington

ISBN 978-0-9852591-5-0

Cover photo of Barbara and Ella Null Warren
Cover design by Richard Mickelson
Formatting by Enterprise Book Services, LLC

Barbara A. Whittington is an award-winning author. Her essays and stories have appeared in The Christian Science Monitor, Cat Fancy Magazine, Woman's World Magazine, World Writer's Magazine Issue #4 - UK, The Cleveland Plain Dealer, The Charleston Gazette, Woman's Voices of Columbus, The Dayton Journal Herald Newspaper and dramatized on British Broadcasting - NPR. Many of the stories have been reprinted.

Dedicated to my daughters - Lisa, Susan, and Jill.

Table of Contents

To Erma Bombeck with Love	1
A Girl from Hometown	3
My Daddy's Eyes	9
High School	15
Becoming a Queen	23
Me and Pattie and the Pink Pill Plane Crash	27
How Long Can a Mother Watch Her Kids Sweat?	33
The County Fair	37
A Rainbow by Choice	41
Glue, Glop and Glitter	43
The Awful Orange-ness	45
Mother Fails to Get the Picture	47
Blundering Bagger	51
School Lunches 1950's Style	53
Call this a Vacation	55
The Seventh Grade Choral Concert	57
Let's Watch the Truck	61
Transportation Special	63
A Letter to School	65
Don't Wish for a Well	69
Hurricane Fran and Lessons Learned	71
Marrying Off the Baby	75
Grandma's Rocking Chair	79
Imperfect Family Makes the Holiday	81
Thanksgiving Poem	83
The Gift of Time	85
On Time	87
Spring Cleaning - Mother's Way	89
Barbara's Fruit n Nut Scones	93
Like My Mother	95
Mother and Me	99
A Special Woman a Special Time	101

A Lonely Christmas	105
The Red Christmas Cane	109
A New Year's Greeting	111
Rakes and Flowers and Memories	115
December 7, 1941	121
Dr. Oz is in My Purse	125
The Little Guy	127
Help Me Make it Through a Month	131
Obama versus McCain	133
Eyebrows: Help	135
Hair Dilemma	137
Oh, I Love a Trip	139
Sad Good Byes	143
The Good Life	147
City Litter Versus Country Litter	151
My Sister Donna Sue	153
Loving Paul	159
Good Bye to Summer	163
In My Mind I'm Always Going Home	167
Bonus Chapters	173
Missing: Sweet Baby James	173
Chapter One	175
Chapter Two	181
Chapter Three	183
Chapter Four	187

"The Lord is my strength and my shield; my heart trusts in him, and he helps me. My heart leaps for joy, and with my song I praise him." Psalm 28:7

To Erma Bombeck with Love

I was motivated to write about family life by the stories written by Erma Bombeck whom I read daily in the Cleveland Plain Dealer newspaper. Her tales let me know I wasn't the only one finding the roles of wife and mother in suburbia less than glamorous. She could turn the events of an ordinary day into a hilarious adventure. Through her, I learned to laugh rather than cry at daily mishaps. Laughter helped the day I was baking cookies and spilled a five pound bag of sugar on the kitchen floor and followed it up with a bowl of eggs.

I figured if she could deal with family life and survive to write about it, I could too. I had the tools: a husband, three precocious daughters, and a ranch house where kids and dogs reigned.

Before we met, I wrote her several letters. Because I so identified with her, I didn't think of her as a famous celebrity. Surprisingly, she wrote back, encouraging me to continue writing. Below is a photo of us at a benefit at Lake Erie College, Painesville, Ohio in April of 1981. As the speaker, she kept the audience in stitches and I became a lifelong fan.

Barbara A. Whittington

Elizabeth Vollstadt, Erma Bombeck,
Barbara Whittington
1982 Lake Erie College

A Girl from Hometown

I was born in Hometown, West Virginia, on June 8, 1945, to Ollie and Cecil Null. I was delivered at home by Dr. Bland and Mrs. Ella Brown, a neighbor who helped birth babies. She and her husband Tom built the first house in Hometown in the 1920's.

Hometown hugs the bank of the Kanawha River in Putnam County between the towns of Red House and Bancroft. Our street rested between the river and the railroad tracks that split the town. Many nights I fell asleep to the whistle of a night train.

Mother and Daddy moved from Putnam County to Raleigh County for daddy to work in the coal mines. After a few years he became seriously ill with lung disease. They moved back to Putnam County to be near family. They had a house built in Hometown beside Aunt Gay and Uncle Hank Boggess.

Daddy's doctor in Charleston sent him to Missouri to see a lung specialist. Daddy took a train to St. Louis. The specialist said daddy was too ill to have more children. They already had Ralph, Maxine, Ella, Donna Sue, and they'd lost Cecil Jr. at nine months to a birth defect.

The doctor told daddy of a simple procedure, a vasectomy, that was fast becoming a means of birth control. So daddy opted for the procedure.

A month or so after he returned from St. Louis mother became pregnant with me. "I wrote to that old doctor in St. Louis," mother told me, "and I gave him a piece of my mind." Evidently daddy had missed the part about not being safe for a number of weeks after the procedure. Even unplanned, I had plenty of love from mother, daddy, and my siblings. After all, I was the baby.

One time when I had an ear infection mother carried me over to see May Wilkinson, a neighbor. Mother said May would blow smoke in an infant's ear and cure the infection. She didn't tell me if the smoke cured mine but I would assume it did.

Daddy ran a cement block plant in Hometown while he was well enough. Daddy bought it from my Uncle Harley, Daddy's brother. Lenard, Harley's son, was driving one of the big heavy trucks for daddy. My brother Ralph was running the plant part time. Lenard told me a few years ago when he asked Ralph for a raise, he fired him. Lenard said, "My own cousin fired me!" A bit of family drama.

Mother went to work at American Viscose during daddy's illness. He would walk to Jackson's Store on the main highway to meet mother at midnight where she was dropped off on week nights when she worked. My cousin, Lenard, said daddy would see him sitting on the railroad track courting his girlfriend, Frankie Brown, and daddy would start to sing the song, "Frankie and Johnny were sweethearts." There weren't many places in Hometown to woo a girl. The railroad track was perfect as long as a train wasn't coming.

When daddy died at age 47, I was two. We had a few rough years I was told. Mother went back to work at American Viscose and I was cared for by Grandma Casto until Sue and Ella came home from school. Ralph and Eunice lived across the street and kept tabs on us.

At the time, mother bought my sister, Sue, a boy's bike so she could pick me up at Grandma's a few streets away and carry me home on the bike's back fender.

Mother married my stepfather when I was five and we moved to Rock Branch, seven miles south of Hometown, to a two-story house on the highway. It had rooms to explore and a large closet off the bedroom I shared with my sister, Sue. That closet became my hide out. It had large windows and I could keep tabs on mother in the backyard, hanging clothes on the line or picking apples from the orchard behind the house. It was the perfect place to spy on the enemy, my stepfather, whom I watched make many trips to the smoke house in the yard. The day there was an explosion in that building, I learned his home brew, or beer, was made, bottled, and stored there.

I got off on the wrong foot with Mr. Bob Bailey, my step father. I'd never been made to eat everything on my plate. That was an important thing for a kid to do in his rule book. When he informed me of his rule during a meal early on, I escaped upstairs to mother who was listening to a radio program on Bob's new mahogany Magnavox television with radio and record player, bought especially for viewing the news of Adlai Stevenson, Bob's candidate in the upcoming presidential election. It was also useful for watching Sky King, Lassie, and Saturday cartoons. Furthermore, I could listen to Elvis records. Oh, Mother's recommendation for mealtime was to always let Bob finish eating first.

I wasn't interested in impressing Bob and he felt the same about me. Though he did ask me repeatedly to call him daddy. I looked at him one day and said smartly, "I would, Mr. Bailey, but, uh, you're not my daddy." Eventually we came to terms with our relationship and were able to exist amicably.

When I was a teen, Mother let me take a Greyhound bus the fifteen miles to Charleston to shop at Lerner's, The Diamond, and Woolworth's.

Sometimes I'd take the bus to Hometown to visit Grandma Casto, who lived alone since Poppy Sam died. Grandma lived in a trailer in Aunt Gay's backyard and she didn't want her wrestling program interrupted. Ever.

I visited with my cousin Sue, her sister Diane, and sometimes her older siblings, Anna and Sissy. Some evenings, Aunt Gay would take Grandma a bowl of ice cream. She refused to accept unless Aunt Gay took the dime she offered. Mother said that dime kept the peace.

So here I am. Barbara Ann Null Whittington, aka Bobbie Ann, born in Hometown, West Virginia. A Hometown girl, plain and simple.

Sue and **Me**

Anna, me, and Sue

Mother and Grandma Casto

My Daddy's Eyes

In the mirror
My daddy's eyes
Stare back at me
Eyes black
Like the coal he mined.
He died -
Lungs thick with black dust
When I was two.
I never had his hand
To guide me
But I still have his eyes
To watch over me.

Daddy, in a dashing cap, holding Ralph, my only brother. Raleigh County, 1920's.

Brenda, and Sue, and my cousin

Brenda, with me, and our dolls. Hometown.
Our house in the background.

Robert "Bob" Bailey, Mother, and me, dressed for a trip to the mountains to visit friends.

Maxine, me, and Ella

High School

My high school years, 1960-1963, were some of the best of my life. I'd like to say my mind was on academics, but that wouldn't be true. My main concern during that time was experimenting with make up and hair and getting to know boys. School was an afterthought.

I spent hours cutting and styling my hair, thinking I'd have a career as a stylist. Girls were wearing pony tails, French twists, or buns. I revered Helene Curtis, the founder of the first hair spray. I practiced styling my mother's hair, not always with success.

News of my semi-talent traveled around the neighborhood and a few people booked hair appointments on Saturday for Sunday church. I earned one dollar each, my first paying job.

I had a childhood sweetheart. We thought we'd be together forever. He was tall and handsome and my mother liked him almost as much as I did. After a few years he found his true soul mate. I fell in love a few more times before I met mine, my forever guy.

Nitro Theatre was the place to go on Saturday afternoons with friends. Parents would take turns driving us. Often we'd stay the entire afternoon and watch the same movies twice. John Wayne was my hero until Elvis came along in *Love Me Tender*. I saw that movie many times, early on, sitting in the floor of the theatre because there were no seats.

One girl in our neighborhood, older than me by a couple of years, let me hang out with her listening to Elvis records after school. Sometimes her parents would take us to the Valley Belle in Nitro to eat lunch on Saturday, and we'd have soda fountain cherry cokes and sandwiches. Sometimes we'd have ice cream. Valley Belle was a local dairy and seemed to carry a million flavors of ice cream.

We'd skate off all those calories at the skating rink in a large tent by the Nitro-St. Albans bridge. Those were the days!

On warm days I'd walk to the cemetery on the hill above our house. I'd read tombstones, amazed by the number of graves stretched out before me. I'd read the epitaphs. "My Angel. My Baby." And "Blessed are the meek." Or "Under the wide and starry sky - I lie."

I took a job as a carhop one summer at the Superman Drive Inn in St. Albans. I took orders from cars at the curbside and delivered food on trays that hooked on the car window. We wore black pants, white Ben Casey blouses, made popular by the TV show, and white tennis shoes. That job was not for the naive. The night I was asked to serve in the dining room was my undoing. In one of the back booths I served a man who exposed himself. He was a local tennis pro and a friend of the manager, who didn't believe me. That was the beginning of the Me Too era for me and the end of my carhop career. I went home upset. Mother called the manager. But to no avail. **Her customer came first.**

High school lunch was usually at the Poca Dot Inn with friends for a hot dog, served with chili and slaw. We ordered Orange Crush to go with it. We'd sit in the booth and watch couples dance to "The Twist" by Chubby Checkers, crooning from the jukebox, with us mouthing the words. My favorite song then was "Can't Help Falling in Love With You", by Elvis. Those days were heavenly in my mind.

A Girl from Hometown

My step father was becoming an unpredictable binge drinker, and after an intense altercation with my mother, I was shipped off to Texas to live with my sister, Sue, and her husband, James "Brownie," while the two sorted their issues. In Beeville, I was enrolled as a sophomore at A. C. Jones High School, not far from the Naval Base where my brother-in-law was stationed. My first time flying left me in New Orleans for hours before my next flight. Not a good place for a kid to be alone, but I ended up fine.

Everything in my life changed that year. Though I loved my sister, I missed my mom. The school was triple the size of Poca High School. I was lost in those long halls and often late to class. I was called a Yankee. My great grandfather did fight in the Civil War for the Union Army. I wondered if news of the end of the war hadn't reached Texas.

I lugged my books around all day up and down those halls because I couldn't open the combination lock on my locker. I'd get lost and drop my books all over the hallway. If nobody stopped to help me pick them up, I'd stoop and scoop them up myself, my face red from embarrassment.

I was sad to miss my second year at Poca High with friends I'd known all my life. Yet, I was getting quite an education. Mexicans filled some of my classes. My West Virginia accent put me at a disadvantage and I was known as the girl who talked funny and said strange words. Some words that caused me issues, I learned to stop using. Poke as in a sack. Pop as in a Coke. Crack as in, "Please crack a window." I quickly learned what was acceptable and what was not. Later on in Cleveland, I had to learn this lesson again. While there were many ethnic groups on my street, there were no other foreigners from West Virginia.

One boy, named Geronimo or Gerry, was interesting. He sat beside me in study hall. He taught me to say, "Quiero Un beso." I want a kiss. We laughed and joked. But, there was no kissing. I learned dating a Mexican was taboo, and frowned on by all my classmates. That was in 1960-1961. Now, that has changed.

Barbara A. Whittington

When I met Patsy and Patricia we became a threesome. We took driver's training class together and got our driver's license at 15. We skipped school one day to drive to Padre Island on the Gulf Coast, where they assured me we would meet boys. Padre Island back then was nothing like the Padre Island of today, which I've learned is a tourist's spot.

That day we were speeding along when Patsy, driving her sister's car, skidded to the side of the road, and jumped out screaming, "Tar-an-tula!" She pointed to the dash. There sat a gargantuan black spider. We sailed out of the car, screeching and running down the highway. I was doubled over in fear.

Eventually one of the girls, much braver than I, swiped the thing out of the car with her shoe. We had no choice but to crawl back in and drive on. I thought I was going to throw up. I'd have walked home right then but I imagined hundreds of tarantulas marching down that lonely highway. My eyes roamed the inside of that car until I was safely home.

It ended up being a cold day at the beach with zero boys. We learned a hard lesson, and went home cold and disappointed. My sister had not given me permission to go. I suffered daily with nightmares. Finally, I confessed what I'd done. Sue seemed delighted about the spider on the dash.

For a short time I had a crush on a young sailor who worked in my brother-in-law's office. He was from Louisiana. I was hooked when he sang and played his guitar, "Have I told you lately that I love you," one afternoon when he came to the house to help with a repair job. The romance in my head was over when I learned as a Mormon he intended to have multiple wives.

Mother and Bob had worked out their differences and I was back home for my junior year at Poca High. There was much adjusting and before I knew it the year was over.

In my senior year, Mrs. Richie was often our substitute teacher for English. She was elderly and frail. She'd give the class an assignment, set her alarm clock for 30 minutes, and settle in with her head on the desk for a nap. She was always sleepy. When she snored I knew she was sound asleep. I'd set her clock to alarm in five minutes. When the alarm clock blared, she'd jump from her chair, grab the clock, and know she'd been pranked. She'd point at the big burly football players in the back of the room and say, "All right, I know one of you boys did this."

They'd point at me and say in unison, "Bobbie did it."

She'd look at me sitting primly in front of her desk and smile. "Oh, no, you don't! Don't even say it. Bobbie would never do that." She'd glare at the boys in the back of the room, and say, "Jerry! Johnny! You do this again and you're in real trouble." Every day that she taught, it happened, and she never knew the truth. Now, I have to live with the guilt, yet I can't help smiling as I remember.

The football coach, Mr. White, taught Government our senior year. On Monday one of us would ask about the game on Friday night. The class was turned into an instant replay. When Mr. White had to be away for one of our exams that year, he left me in charge. Of both the exam and the answers. I did have a good grade in the class, but still.

After all these years, I count those classmates among my very best friends.

The summer before my senior year, I met my husband, Raymond. We married a few months later. When I graduated I enrolled in beauty school in Charleston. I couldn't tolerate the smell of hair products when I got pregnant a few months in. Thus, ended my beauty career. Something tells me it might have ended early anyway. I had cut Hedy's hair, my brunette mannequin, almost bald the first week. It was then I realized her hair was to be cut in short increments until I could give a proper hair cut. I never did learn. As proven by my children's hair cuts for school pictures.

We moved to the Eastside of Cleveland when Lisa was nine months old. R worked at GM for twenty years. When the Coit Road plant closed he was transferred to Detroit, having done a short stint at the Hamilton plant in Cincinnati the summer before. GM bought our house. We bought a house in Farmington Hills but lived there only a few months.

Barbara A. Whittington

A job opened for R in the Columbus plant, which we'd both prayed for since it was closer to our parents in West Virginia. He left me to sell the house and move in June when school was out.

When we first bought a house in the Cleveland suburbs, I noticed I sounded different from my neighbors, a repeat of what I went through in Texas. My neighbors noticed it too and often made comments. Some were well meaning. Others were not. Our neighborhood was made up of many ethnic groups and I collected a new group of lifelong friends.

While the three children were still home I enrolled in college. I'd always wanted to be a writer, but never thought it possible. The longer I studied the more I realized my options were endless.

I started sending out essays and selling op-ed pieces to big city newspapers. I've learned and keep learning that anything is possible with hard work. With age comes wisdom. Some from books, most from life.

My husband and I had a long marriage with three daughters and eight grandchildren. Though he's gone, I still feel married to him, the man I fell in love with at age seventeen.

Poca High School, Poca, WV

Ray on Trigger - Me on Pearl

Becoming a Queen

When I ran for Queen in grade school I had no inkling how it worked. I knew it was an honor. The King and Queen were crowned during the school carnival, a fun fall event with games and prizes. Candidates placed jars with their photos in local stores. People voted by putting money into the jar. As a kid I didn't realize that one's family could fill the jar and buy the position. I won the title several times along with handsome young men over the years and thought everyone in school liked me. Eventually, I realized that wasn't the case. My step father had bought the title for me and the little bit of glory that went with it. I loved being a queen for a day. But I'm no longer a fan of short lived glory or titles bought in grade school.

Barbara A. Whittington

Danny and Me
King and Queen

A Girl from Hometown

I played Annie Oakley, the woman sharp shooter, in the school play. I got the part not because I was good at speaking or learning lines but because I happened to have the outfit and a cap pistol which was needed to shoot a piece of paper in two. The paper may have already been cut by the teacher before the shooting took place.

Me and Pattie and the Pink Pill Plane Crash

At 4 a.m. this morning, Pattie, my best friend in school, and I were in a plane crash. Don't panic. Relax. We're safe! It's almost 8 a.m. now and I'm sitting on my sofa drinking a cup of Green Mountain coffee and writing this event just as it happened in my dream.

Pattie and I have never been on a plane together. If we had it would be the best plane ride ever. All we have to do is look at each other and we smile. We used to burst out laughing but now that we're old, we just smile. We had so much fun in school. Either playing pranks, getting the boys in trouble, or gossiping. Nearly every day, the teacher would call out, "Bobbie and Pattie, move your seats apart. Now! And stop that talking!" Like talking was bad. I guess she didn't see the laughing. So at the end of each day I'd be up front in my little wooden desk near the teacher and Pattie would be in back, or the other way around and neither of us was laughing.

Last night I got up to get a drink at 3:15, having no idea that I was about to have this incredible journey with Pattie. I got back into my warm bed and curled into a fetal position. Now, it's very painful to get out of bed in the morning because my bones are not fetal friendly anymore. But off I drifted.

Lately I haven't slept well nor do I dream much, and certainly I do not have fun dreams featuring Pattie and me. However this one was not completely fun.

Recently my doctor had recommended a tiny pink pill to help me unclench my jaw at night. It's been clenched for two months. At 10 p.m. that night, like a good patient, I took one of the pink pills. Then, there we were, me and Pattie flying through the friendly skies, attendants up front showing us how to inflate the life vests in case we fell into the water. I remember hoping not to come into contact with water. I can only swim three feet at a time. Next they showed us how to use the oxygen equipment that falls from the ceiling in case the plane loses air pressure. I'm positive that neither Pattie nor I would know how to operate any of those items. We mostly like fun things.

We were not really paying attention to the attendants. We were deciding which uniform to wear. Yes, we had been issued attendant uniforms. Go figure!

Once dressed and in the air we learned that we had to stop in Chicago on our way to Charleston. For some reason, neither Pattie nor I wanted to stop in Chicago. We were running up and down the aisle of the plane complaining and talking when we noticed we were going down, not anywhere near an airport. Like just dropping through midair. Fast.

I ran and buckled myself into a seat beside one of the passengers. I'm sure it was not where I was supposed to be sitting. However, it was the closest seat to the exit and I was taking no chances. I wanted to be saved.

Meanwhile Pattie had decided she could no longer tolerate her uniform, and not really believing we were going down, she had gone in search of something cute to wear.

An expensive carry-on had fallen at her feet. Right away she was oohing and cooing over this red sequined number inside the bag. The next thing I knew she came prancing out of the rest room wearing the outfit. Red. With sequins. I had to admit it really jazzed up her look. Plus, it was that particular red that goes well with dark hair.

The ride down seemed to be going smoothly until the plane hit, oh no, water! I remember calling out, "Oh Jesus. No." I may have said something else but since I'm not totally sure I'll leave that out.

Not one thing fell off the plane and nothing burst into flames. I was shaking from head to toe. My heart was beating like ninety. I don't remember anyone screaming. Yet nobody was joyful either except Pattie who had fallen into a seat beside a rock star wanna be from the 80's. Luckily the jazzy outfit had come with a pair of red backless stilettos. She was dangling one on her toe.

The next thing I knew someone was pulling the plane through the water with a barge like the ones that carry coal on the Kanawha River. It could have been some kind of pontoon. I'm not up on boats. And wouldn't you know it, I woke up and nearly fell out of bed. When my feet hit the floor, I realized it had been a dream and I had to leave all that fun behind.

I have to admit, I'm sleeping better now, my jaw is unclenched, my neck isn't stiff and my stomach is no longer in knots. I wonder how long the doctor will want me to stay on those tiny pink pills? Forever? One can only hope!

Maybe tonight, I'll take a cruise. Pattie might even show up.

Joyce, Grova, Sue, me, Pattie, and Barbara

Tour of old war plane during field trip to Charleston Airport - Far left Pattie, Shirley, Me, Linda, and Karen in doorway of plane.

How Long Can a Mother Watch Her Kids Sweat?

Our best friends got a pool. Then our next door neighbor got one. Now, we, too, have a pool. How long can a decent mother watch her kids sweat?

At the store the kids squealed for an in-the-ground pool, the deluxe model with a diving board, wide sweeping steps, and a gigantic slide.

What we came home with was an above-the-ground pool, the economy model that, in the words of the clever sales man, "You install it yourself in a few short hours."

As the smooth talking young man further explained to my husband, "You just lift the sod where the pool will be placed, spread a little sand, put down the track, roll on the sides, add the liner, water, kids and presto. Instant pool party."

Yeah right. I should have seen through him the minute he handed over that instruction booklet three inches thick.

Too soon we learned that with the sod had to come a little earth - 18 inches to be exact. Not only did we find that our lawn wasn't level where the 20-foot round pool was going to set, we learned that this was not a one-man job, and we didn't have many friends.

Eventually, though, the track was in place. Leveling the patio blocks wasn't so difficult either. Somehow, we missed the section on bolting the supports to the patio blocks. Maybe it was in Spanish at the back of the book.

That problem finally corrected, the sides rolled onto the track like a charm. A few close friends helped. Okay, so they were blood relatives demanding pool memberships.

We were soon down to installing the filter. The one that came with the deal looked far too sophisticated for a pool that was blue and had dolphins racing around the sides. We studied the filter from all angles.

Hours passed and finally a young fellow stepped from the gathering crowd. What followed was like a scene from "Touched by an Angel."

With ease the young guy read the blueprints, even pronouncing the technical terms. He connected the "A" parts to the "B" parts without benefit of the sledgehammer my husband offered.

When the filter started to purr, the crowd cheered. Nothing could go wrong now. We paid the water delivery guy hundreds of dollars for water and treated it with hundreds of dollars worth of chemicals. We sighed as the kids jumped into their new bathing suits.

"Wait," our youngest child screeched, "where are the beach balls and rafts?"

"Yeah," our middle child picked up the cry. "What about the floating lounge chairs, the goggles, and the fins?"

"Hold on," our oldest yelled, sitting up on her beach towel where she'd been lathering on tanning lotion, "you forgot the basketball set."

It seems that their best friends have all those things. So does our neighbor.

Now I wish someone would ask me how long a decent mother should watch her kids sweat.

Jill Marie proving that the Whittington's needed a pool.

The County Fair

When my children were growing up, the highlight of our summer was attending the Geauga County Fair in Burton, Ohio. It was dubbed by our children as "the greatest fair anywhere!"

My own experience with fairs left me less enthusiastic. I grew up on the West Virginia State Fair at Lewisburg. It seemed a continent away from our home in the Kanawha Valley. The ride up into the mountains always made me sick.

In the backseat of our fifties Ford sedan, I would hang my dizzy little head, with its Buster Brown haircut, into the front seat and moan.

"Well, I've never been carsick a day in my life," my mother declared, rolling her eyes upward. It seemed that neither had anyone else in the car. Certainly not my sister, Sue, or her friend, Mary Kay. They were ten going on twenty-one that summer and had BOYS on their minds. Nobody understood the malady that had stricken the five-year old.

Once we arrived at the fair, it took me the whole day to recover. Then, it was back into the car for the trip home.

I didn't enjoy one thing about that fair. Not the cotton candy. Not plucking the yellow duck out of the water. Not even winning the monkey-on-a-stick.

My kids were lucky. The road leading to the Geauga County Fair was flat compared to that West Virginia mountain terrain.

On the drive to Burton, the only thing we had to contend with was the long line of cars driven by the "foreigners." Yes, those Clevelanders thirsting for knowledge of the country. We'd approach Rt. 87 in Russell and there they were, making their way to farm country where they'd wade in large packs through barns to stare at the largest pig and fanciest rooster, and to watch the milking machine deliver Big Bertha of her load of milk.

The Cadillacs, New Yorkers, and Thunderbirds were interspersed with horse-drawn Amish buggies. My family would bring up the rear in our gray Nova. We'd come racing into line from our subdivision in Chesterland. In those days we were always rushing. Forever late. Forever forgetting something. A shoe. A comb. A kid.

Our children were basically fair-deprived in our pastel environment. It was the late sixties. The houses lining our streets were pink, blue, or yellow.

"We don't have enough land to raise a 4-H animal," I fibbed to the children each year, as we trudged through the barns. Poor lambs. They bought every word. These children also lived in a house where the mother couldn't sew. Well, she could sew, just not anything recognizable. Certainly she had no skills worthy of passing on to a child who might be seeking a fair ribbon.

When we reached Burton, we'd inch our way around the square. We'd pay to park and belly the Nova up onto someone's front lawn, wedging it between another car and a cement lawn ornament.

The kids would race through the gate straight to the midway. They'd try to see who could rid themselves the quickest of the allowance clutched in their sweaty little palms. Rides, sideshows, and games. We always had a good 15 minutes before we'd have to shell out a loan.

My husband was reeled in by the tractor display. His eyes would light up at the sight of all those mammoth machines. In his best plaid shirt, a package of Red man wedged in the back pocket of his jeans, he'd be drawn like a magnet to the John Deere tractors. He'd stare until his eyes would glaze over. Then he'd realize his decision had been made, not in favor of a John Deere. He'd opted instead for the mortgage on that pastel house. He'd move slowly from the tractors to the displays. He'd visit the largest potato, largest pumpkin, and largest sunflower. For hours he'd peruse the biggest and best of what Geauga County had to offer.

I made my way to the tent where the politicians held court. There I collected pens, and had my hand shaken by every potential office holder. I felt special. Needed. Especially by those running for office in our county. I usually walked away with an eight pack of Pepsi, and a blue ribbon that said, "You're Number One."

I visited the jellies, the jams, the pies, the cakes. Fancy confections that would make anyone proud. I visited countless buildings that housed all the other arts at which I did not excel.

Eventually the family would reunite. We'd trip over to see the horse pulling contest, the Amish buggy race, the fattest woman, the tallest man, the half-man half-snake, the world's smallest horse, and the man who lived in a jar.

We'd stuff ourselves with corn dogs. Cotton candy. Elephant ears. Fried pies. Hoagies.

On the way home, we'd sing, "Ninety-nine bottles of beer on the wall." I'd pop a Tums and loosen my belt.

We decided that no matter where we live our very own county fair is the greatest fair anywhere.

A Rainbow by Choice

I should have been addressing the business letters that had to be mailed that afternoon. Instead I was scrubbing crayon off the kitchen table. As I finished the chore, my six-year-old daughter proudly handed me her picture for inspection. There, in a kaleidoscope of bright colors, was her world. A mother, a father, and three children stood in front of a slightly lopsided white ranch house, surrounded by dozens of pink and purple flowers. Everyone was smiling, even the big, yellow sun overhead.

Seeing my daughter's excitement, I realized that her life stands before her as inviting and unspoiled as the large sheets of paper on which she draws. Just as she selects the colors for her pictures, she will make decisions that will form the pattern of her life. I hope she chooses as carefully as she chooses from the array of colored crayons in her box.

I looked back on the colors of my world, marriage and dinner by candlelight, baby bottles, fancy home-baked cookies, car pools, the roller rink in winter and the duck pond in the summer.

As the children grew, books, newspapers and magazines entered and filled my days. I began to learn new things. The promise that someday I'd write began to take the shape of a daily journal. Before long it was poetry, an essay, a story. I enrolled as a part-time student at the local community college. My youngest daughter accompanied me. While I was in English, she was downstairs with the other toddlers in Early Learning, discovering that fingers make better designs than paint brushes. Her Snoopy book bag was heavier than mine.

Overcoming one hurdle after another, I stopped thinking of giant steps and measured my success by my good feelings. When my writing was praised by an instructor, I sent an essay to a large city newspaper. It was published. So was another and another. My motto is still one course at a time.

I may never get a degree or I may get one when I'm old and gray. It doesn't matter. What matters is that I feel good. I run my life according to the things that are important to me. I chose my family first and my career second. I often restore order to the kitchen instead of going to my desk to write.

The three girls grumbled first about pitching in, but found that some of the old rules have been relaxed. They started concocting interesting dishes. The only rule is that food has to be edible and they have to clean up afterwards.

My husband seems to take great pride in my writing and his family.

We are all learning. The colors in my world are varied and of different hues and they seem to harmonize, even though there are some smudges here and there.

My youngest daughter continues to share her world with me through her pictures. If sometimes she misses the paper with her crayon I know it's because she's like her mother. She's still learning.

Glue, Glop and Glitter

When our youngest daughter went to nursery school it went well for both of us. While I was busy learning the art of carpooling, holding six hands and balancing three wet paintings, she was busy learning the art of showing and telling, showing all the right things and telling all the wrong ones.

When I went to a meeting to sign her up for next year, I knew I was going to need more than an initial orientation to get into the swing of things.

I realize that four-year olds are more advanced now, but changing classes seemed a bit much. That threw me even in high school.

As an occasional helper, I will be there clearing a path from class to class as she paints her fingers, glues her clothes and glitters the room.

This year all the groups are sharing snack time. Even if I have a good day, where am I going to get a recipe that's simple to make, serves forty-two, and can be eaten on a toothpick?

I foresee problems. I had trouble last year baking cupcakes and pouring juice for fourteen. Scraping up the crumbs was no picnic either.

One possible way to have my daughter attend this excellent program but by pass the helper bit may be for me to enroll as a student.

The requirements, besides tuition, are that one must be 3 years of age or older, potty-trained, and secure enough to meet the outside world.

Oh, well. I can't swing another tuition anyway, so I'll get out the Rice Krispies and marshmallows. Perhaps by the time she goes to kindergarten, I will have forgotten all this.

After pulling my first day of duty, I have only enough strength to say, "Make that high school."

Two of the carpoolers who survived nursery school and the carpooling. Jill with Stevie, best friends.

The Awful Orange-ness

When I was invited to spend a week with my sister, Sue, in Florida, I knew I couldn't arrive looking like a snowflake from northeast Ohio. I might act like a mother who has never been on vacation without her children when I hit the waves with the inflated alligator around my waist, but must I be pointed at and labeled as one who survived the blizzard of 1978 in Cleveland?

I had to have a tan. I wanted the real thing this year. Last year I went the route of the bottle tan and had orange elbows and knees for weeks. For days I watched the rain pour down and felt a little like Noah. I don't have a dove, but I do have staying power. When I awoke one morning to sunshine, I dashed out onto the patio with my towel and lotion. I was desperate. Vacation time was drawing near. I didn't have time for a gradual tan.

Whoever recommended the thirty-minutes on each side a day evidently lives in a tropical climate. Here, you get it while you can.

After five minutes the sun disappeared behind a cloud. I stayed outside. Even when the temperature dropped and the wind whipped up, I wasn't deterred. I've heard you can tan on cloudy days, but this was getting ridiculous.

It took all my strength to hold the towel down and the rain was beginning to splash all around me.

I gave up when the kids called me inside to read the storm warning on the television.

Two days later when I saw the sun again, I got excited. We were invited to use a neighbor's pool, and after packing enough food and gear for a three day trip, we headed next door. The sun danced on the brilliant blue water, and I could already see myself stepping out of my beach robe in Florida to glances of envy.

As I chased kids in and out of the pool, and in and out of the bathroom, I debated the necessity of a tan for the beach. Basking in the sun for two-minute stretches didn't seem to do the trick, and neither did serving lunch on a covered patio.

I ended up with beautifully tanned arms and shoulders, a tanned face with white circles around the eyes where sun glasses had been, and white legs.

I have decided either to tan as I go, and hang my legs out of the plane window, or shop for a bathing suite that has legs to the ankle.

I plan to invite my sister here for a winter vacation. I wonder how she will look in a snow suit?

Mother Fails to Get the Picture

When my children brought home their school pictures, I cringed.

These kids can leave home looking cherubic, but the minute they pose for that school photographer they are transposed into unrecognizable beings.

My middle daughter brought home pictures bearing her name and room number that couldn't have been my offspring, nor even a distant relative.

I had worked for hours on this child. Her hair was parted in the middle and drawn into a cute little ponytail over each ear. Even though she is at an awkward age, she looked adorable when she went out that door. Her missing front teeth only added to her charm.

The kid in this picture has her mouth open wide displaying ugly dark gaps. Her one visible ponytail is lopsided, her part uneven, and her bangs look like they were cut with pinking shears.

I know this isn't my child because I always give my children a good haircut before school pictures.

The only thing vaguely familiar is the red sweater the child has on. My daughter has one, too, but hers isn't covered with ink spots.

Barbara A. Whittington

Our school seems to hire photographers that snap all their pictures after gym, art, recess, or lunch. Why they can't take those pictures as the kids climb aboard the school bus in the morning is beyond me.

I don't mind my children having the wind-blown look. However, I dislike passing around pictures that present them as survivors of a tornado.

Next year I hope the photographer can keep his records straight and send home pictures that properly portray my children. If not, then I hope he takes up retouching.

Susan's school picture - Hair style by mom.

Blundering Bagger

Without any previous academic training, I hold the title of The World's Worst Lunch Maker. At least I was so voted by my family.

My husband thought the knack of making lunches came with the package deal when we exchanged vows. He even thought that time would improve my talent, but he concedes now that I'm still on the bottom.

My titled is undaunted by the splendid selection I offer. It seems to be the way I put things together that turns this group off.

Can I help it if the pickles that went with the egg salad got shipped out with the peanut butter? And the jelly just happened to ride out on top of the salami?

I just make the lunches and put them in their designated spots in the refrigerator. What they do after I close the door is their own business.

It isn't easy producing creative lunches to the tune of Saturday Night Fever on the stereo, the Brady Bunch on television, and Silent Night being played on the piano?

The kids refuse lunch money saying school lunches are hazardous to their health, and besides, they might be nutritious.

I've tried letting them make their own lunches, but a quick check into the fat bags being carried out the door turns up nothing but Ho Ho's and Twinkie's.

Last week I found out that we can claim a new dependent on our income tax this year. A man at work has been eating my husband's lunch for the past 10 years.

Though there isn't much competition for my title, I may lose it in the next election.

Today when the kids checked the school menu, grabbed their peanut butter and salami sandwiches, and headed out the door I heard them mutter, "This sure beats noodles and gravy over biscuits. "They're called Grandma's Biscuits. Ha! Those things never saw a grandma!"

School lunches 1950's Style

Back when school lunches were made from scratch in the school kitchen, my friends and I loved the spaghetti and meat balls, and the vegetable soup served with peanut butter and honey sandwiches. Those really were the good old days. When the cooks were personable and some were even neighbors. Here's some of the friends I shared those good times with in the school lunch room. Many of us went from grade one to grade twelve together, and marched in unison all the way to graduation day.

Barbara A. Whittington

Rock Branch Elementary Class 1953-1954 Grade 3

Call this a Vacation!

I'm beginning to wonder why they call it summer vacation. It supposedly started in June, but I'm still waiting for it to hit.

I can think of other things to call this time span between June and September, when the kids are underfoot, under the table, and everywhere else, but vacation is not one of them.

My dictionary tells me that vacation means freedom from activity, a rest, respite or intermission. Something tells me I'm not experiencing a summer vacation.

The kids may be having one, as they rise every morning to greet the dawn and retire when the hoot owls are exhausted. I am not.

They change outfits as often as Marie Osmond and eat twice their weight in food each day. Otherwise they're totally bored.

When I think of vacation, I see myself sleeping past 7:00 a.m, and not having to face Toasty Postys. I dream of having my meals served to me, and of reading all those best sellers stashed in my closet before they turn yellow and brittle.

Our yard does resemble a resort area with beach towels, tennis rackets, and drinking glasses scattered about, but a groundskeeper does not arrive each morning to clean up nor does a waiter appear to refill glasses.

Maybe that's why our kitchen looks like a deli with the array of food on its counter. It's a cross between a deli and a fast food joint. However, I don't get to leave when they're finished eating.

Just because our freezer is stocked with hamburger patties and pie tarts doesn't mean I am in competition with the golden arches or trying to see how many I can serve a day.

Yesterday when the washer broke down, the kids took a bath in lime gelatin, and the dog ran away, I knew I couldn't take much more. All that saved me was a quick glance at the calendar, and the thankful knowledge that I am not a school teacher.

Neighborhood gang on Cherry Lane

The Seventh Grade Choral Concert

There were over a dozen outfits scattered on the frilly pink bedspread and my daughter was in tears. Smashing Pumpkins was wailing about love at a volume already proven to cause deafness in rats.

She has nothing to wear. Her dress is too short. Her skirt is too tight. Her best pants are in the laundry and the other ten outfits have similar flaws. Maybe she'll stay home. She looks in the mirror. Her hair isn't right anyway. Besides, if she's not allowed to wear make-up she'll look dead next to the other seventh grade girls.

It's the most horrible, terrible, awful night of her entire life.

It's the night of the seventh grade choral concert.

No. She isn't doing a solo. She isn't even standing in the front row. She's buried somewhere behind the broad shoulders of Jimmie Johnson and another not so small girl. She's got the jitters just the same.

"Great!" Kari, my daughter's best friend, storms into the backseat when we swing by her house. "I'm never talking to that woman again!" She gets into the back seat, slamming the car door, and holds her hand to her head as if she might faint. I knew that woman was her mother.

Not only did Kari's mother insist on zippering her into this perfectly awful ugly flowered dress, which was, by the way, too short, but she insisted on taking pictures. Guess where? Kari sinks lower into the seat. "On the front lawn! With all the neighbors watching. She took not one picture, but a dozen. I had to stand beside her new birdbath."

To make matters worse, right that minute, the dress was cutting off the circulation in Kari's arms.

"I don't feel like singing," Kari moans, moving around restlessly. "I think I'm going to be sick." She presses herself back against the leather seat and holds her hand to her mouth.

"Don't you dare be sick," my daughter threatened. "Not in my dad's new car!"

"I wish I'd stayed home." Kari sighed. "I really do. So," she says, "what do you think Tammy will wear?"

I can see Kari in the rear view mirror. She's relaxing a bit.

"Something extravagant," my daughter gushes. "Something cool. Maybe her black leather pants and that sparkly purple top."

Kari wails again.

"What about Sherri?" My daughter asks. "Think she'll wear that blouse cut down to here?"

"I hope not." Kari is thoroughly disgusted. "The boys will act stupid. They won't be able to sing. Harry Kink will fall off the stage."

"The boys can't sing anyway. Look at Derek. He sounds like a girl on his solo. Of course, he doesn't sound froggy like that nerd Rob."

"We don't sound any better, you know." Kari folds her arms tightly against her chest. "I wish my mother had never made me join the stupid choir. I hate it."

"I do too," my daughter adds, patting Kari on the arm.

We are turning into the school parking lot.

"Look! There's Miss Tanya Straight A's. She's with, oh no!" Kari squeals, and jumps up and down in the backseat, "It's Richard-Know-It-All."

"Throw up!" My daughter says, craning her neck to see the two kids on the sidewalk.

"Gross!" Kari sits up straighter.

I hear the window being rolled down as I pull into a parking space.

"Hey, Tanya!" Kari calls loudly.

"Hi, Richard!" My own daughter's sweet voice rings out, "Wait up. We'll walk in together."

The Seventh Grade Choral Concert. I wouldn't miss it for the world.

Let's Watch the Truck

When my husband bought a pick up truck, I had no idea I would end up in the back seat. I don't know what went wrong. He didn't act this way when we bought a car.

I hope there is a time limit, or at least a money back guarantee on his fascination.

We used to spend our evenings watching television, together, but now we spend them watching the truck.

At first, I supported the situation and served coffee to the hordes of male friends who gathered in our driveway. After a few days, I tired of hearing the pros and cons of four wheel drive and posi traction and posted myself behind the living room drapes. I figured he would eventually miss me.

I should have known there would be problems, the first day he climbed aboard the truck. He melted into the decor and looked as though he had arrived from the factory in it.

I expected his admiration of this thing to be high because he waited so long to get it, but I didn't expect my blood pressure to rise too.

Last week my husband said the truck proved its worth when it hauled our mini television to the repair shop. I guess every television needs its own conveyance.

I used to enjoy an occasional Sunday drive, but we ride in this vehicle so much that I have developed saddle sores. I knew I was dealing with a mother bear protecting her cub when I complained that the seats were hard. He told me if the seats were a problem that home wasn't a long walk.

Yesterday we took it in for a six week check up and I felt like I was escorting a new baby to the pediatrician. I expected the garage attendant to come out with a stethoscope around his neck and a needle to start its shots.

I've decided it must be the red color of this thing that has him so enthralled. I know it isn't the price he paid for it or the gas mileage it gets.

Men watching their trucks through the ages.

Transportation Special

Shopping for a used car last week, I overheard my husband telling the man at the car dealer he definitely didn't want a car previously owned by a sales person or a stay at home mom. I was close enough to catch the sarcasm.

Putting a mother in the same category as a sales person is a bit absurd. Even if he did take a survey of the cars traded in by both, and did find them in an equal state of disrepair, I dislike the comparison.

It's not true that mothers get out of their cars ONLY when the gas tank is empty, not if they have a credit card.

He swears my own driving habits are crazy. I can't help it if the only hairdresser that can control my cowlick moved forty miles north, and the only store that carries my favorite brand of coffee is now in the next county.

I suspect that this man would buy a car that was driven by a nationwide sales guy before he would buy one driven by a mother of three like me. At least, he says, there wouldn't be apple cores and half-eaten hot dog buns under the seats.

Chances are a sales person never had to drive hungry children across town after school to the orthodontist.

Though I will admit I'm guilty of serving food in the car, I can't accept responsibility for the many miles the car carries. I didn't drive seventy miles to find the right breed of hunting dog. I also didn't drive fifty miles to pick up an outdated tractor part. I suffer in silence.

When I picked up 15 homemade pies and delivered them to a school social, he got all worked up. Just because a lemon meringue pie hit the floor when I rounded the corner to school is no reason to fall apart. I expected the number of fatalities to be much higher.

He came home yesterday with a used car for me. He bought it from a little old woman, he said. He doesn't know, but she delivers the daily newspaper, the yearly telephone books, and has just received an award from Avon for covering the largest territory in the state.

All of this was accomplished in the little sedan now sitting in our driveway. At least there are no apple cores or hot dog buns to clean out.

A Letter to School

Dear School:

Will you please excuse my daughter for being absent yesterday? She said she was sick.

She did look pale until the school bus left, and then she began to rally. Her condition seemed to worsen as she settled down beneath an afghan to watch a morning talk show that featured Andy Gibb.

When he appeared on stage, she started to moan. I know her ailment, if not original, is authentic.

Her temperature shot up two degrees, and I ordered her to bed. She felt so bad that I wheeled the television into her room. Her condition stabilized after the show went off, and she regained her appetite.

Poor thing. I thought I could take her to school at noon, but while she was having some clear broth, Donny Osmond came on the screen.

Well, she had a relapse and had to be tucked in again. Even under the covers she continued to chill, and her lips turned blue. I had never witnessed anything quite like it. I wanted to tell you the strange symptoms of this unique affliction in case anyone else at school comes down with it.

Barbara A. Whittington

Though she will be back in school today, swinging her purse and looking completely normal, she evidently is prone to fad-type diseases and should be watched.

This particular sickness does have a temporary cure. She was back to her usual self, after the television went on the blink, the record albums were hidden and the poster of Andy and Donny taken off the walls.

Please let me know if I can be of any help to other distressed parents.

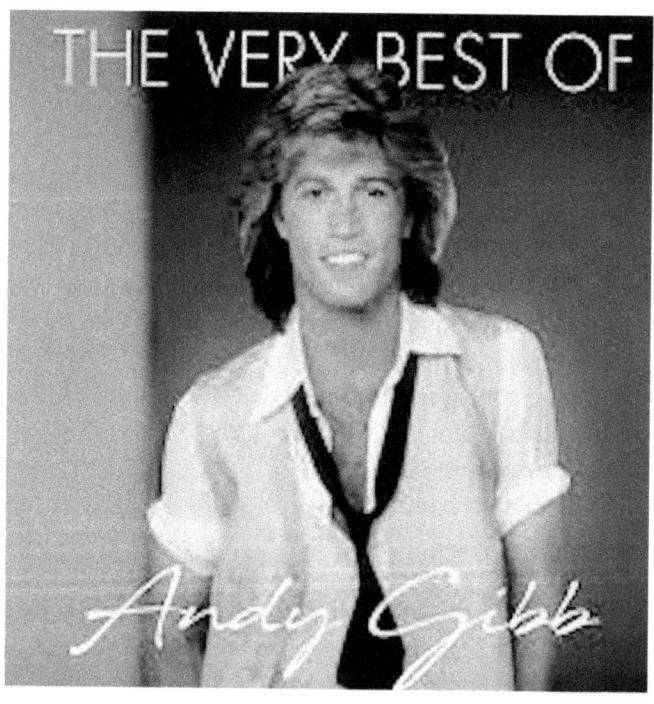

Andy Gibb

Donny Osmond

Don't Wish for a Well

A benefit of country living is the unique water system. We call ours a well. For several years we drank and washed from what we thought was an endless supply of free water.

Eventually we installed a sophisticated water softener. What the heck. We didn't pay water bills. We could afford to get the red out. The softener ate a bag of salt pellets a month and only made itself known when guests arrived.

When the old pump started sounding like a freight train, we replaced it with a noiseless submersible kind. "Might as well put new pipes in the well while I'm here," the technician said, "and you'll be all set."

We were until our neighbor drilled a new well close by. I had heard of the water tables changing, but this was ridiculous.

We had to drill a new deeper well with a larger pump and more new pipes. We needed a new lawn also but we had water.

"Just don't drink it until you get it tested by the health department," the friendly well driller yelled as he pulled out with my fat check in his hand.

The procedure to purify a new well is simple," the agent from the health department said. "Sterilize a garden hose by pouring a cup of bleach through it. Pour two gallons of bleach into the well. Hook the hose to the outside faucet, and run water into the well for 30 minutes. Turn all the inside faucets on until you smell bleach. Don't use the water for 24 hours."

For six weeks the agent took samples and the reports came back unsafe. When I wasn't throwing bleach into the well, I was boiling water to drink.

The kids acquired a taste for lukewarm Kool-Aid. After each report, they made another gallon.

We could use the chlorinated water for baths if we wore nose clips, and I could do the laundry if we wanted to lighten it two shades.

After I had badgered the agent about my boiling, he offered to send out enough red dye to color Chagrin River.

"We'll check for surface water contamination," he said. "Your husband must dig a two foot moat around the well casing. Pour in the dye and let the water hose trickle into that for 12 hours. Call me if your water turns pink or red. Sometimes new wells have to be treated 12 times to make them safe."

I thought I'd heard it all.

That night in the dark, my husband dug the moat, poured in the dye and started the hose. The next afternoon I received a letter from the health department. Our water was safe, had indeed been safe before my last call. The report just hadn't been read.

I can't enjoy a drink from that faucet, though, until I figure out how to siphon the pool that is spreading all over my backyard from the rain. It looks a lot like the Chagrin River, only it's red.

Hurricane Fran and Lessons Learned
Sept. 5, 1996

The year my husband made a motion to forego fall window washing for a trip to North Carolina, I quickly seconded. Corn was still head-tall on the farm down the road, but birds were beginning to migrate south. I knew winter wasn't far off. A mini vacation was what we needed. Besides other family in North Carolina, there was a new grandson we'd never seen.

Hurricane Fran was nothing more than a storm churning in the Atlantic when we left our home in Ohio, so we meandered along, enjoying the sunny days and stopping often to browse in antique shops.

Relatives warned us, when we made a stop in West Virginia, that Fran was moving toward the coastline and that we should turn back, but, the skies were a beautiful blue and there was a new Barbie doll and a fire truck in the trunk and they would not deliver themselves. Too, Snooper's Antique Mall wasn't that far ahead.

When we stopped for the night in Fancy Gap, Virginia, the innkeeper informed us that the night before rooms had been filled with people fleeing Hurricane Fran. He raised his eyebrows when we said we were headed south. Over chili dogs at the Mayberry Diner, we were entertained by locals telling hurricane stories.

That night, we watched the news and that's when worry set in. Fran was due in our daughter's neighborhood any minute and there we were in Virginia unable to stop the storm or to help in any way.

After a long night without sleep, we learned that Fran had indeed swept through our daughter's community. Thankfully, she was able to let us know that she and her family were safe.

We watched the news and debated staying put. The morning that had started out bright and sunny was now black. Rain came down in sheets. The lights in the Inn went out. Then the television flickered off.

There was nothing to do but head south to Fort Bragg. Before we could leave, our phone went dead and there was no longer running water in the bathroom.

We started to mush on. We had toys to deliver, and, most of all, there was family who needed us.

Due to flash floods we stayed on the interstate rather than take side roads as we often did. Rain was still coming down in sheets and the wind had picked up. Stopping in Winston-Salem for breakfast, we were blown from our car to McDonald's door.

As we drove further south, we began to view the devastation and damage left in Fran's wake. Twisted outbuildings. House trailers crumpled by huge trees. Siding ripped from homes. Trees uprooted with eight to ten feet of earth clinging to them.

Finally we arrived in our daughter's neighborhood where downed trees were everywhere and debris covered all the street signs.

They had no power. No water. No phones, but the sight of our car pulling into the driveway put a smile on our daughter's face and tears of relief in my eyes. We had brought them more than gifts. We'd brought them a mom and a dad, a grandma and grandpa.

Without the air conditioner it was hot and the adults complained continuously but the children thrived on it. Our granddaughter set up a Barbie village with some of her friends. They gave all the dolls a ride on the new town fire truck, graciously shared by our infant grandson who slept peacefully in his crib. Before long, grandpa was assessing the damage in the yard. With his help the backyard fence was soon fixed and all the tree limbs and debris removed. Neighbors helped each other as they worked with chain saws and hauled away debris.

We needed water and ice but learned the whole town was without both. No electricity meant no television or radio, and that meant no news. Rumors, however, were plentiful.

"There's ice at the BP on Raeford Road." So we drove in that direction only to find a no ice sign.

"There's ice at the mini mart on Fayetteville Road." Off we went again, and found the same disappointing sign. Finally, we gave up. We bought juice, snacks, and wet wipes.

With no refrigeration, we worried about the baby's formula and shared our concern with a neighbor. Soon we had a large bag of ice for the cooler from the Ft. Bragg Officer's Club finagled by a friend.

For dinner there was nothing to do but go for pizza. A closed sign greeted us where the window of Papa John's Pizza used to be. Pizza Hut was filled to capacity. However, at Domino's our order was quickly taken. There, we found ten employees tossing dough, slathering sauce, and adding condiments. All their employees had shown up to pull storm duty, even those not scheduled. The human spirit was alive and well.

We were happy to take cold showers by candlelight. Later, we all sat outside on the dark porch and got to know the neighbors as they walked around and shared disaster stories.

When hundreds of lights in the neighborhood flickered on a cheer went up that echoed through the streets.

The next morning at McDonald's, the line was out the door but no one complained. It had the atmosphere of a big coffee klatch with everyone talking to everyone else, an anomaly in today's society.

It was sobering to see what Fran had done as we watched the storm damage on television.

In Wrightsville Beach, one resident sitting on a mattress in her yard offered a summation. "All we lost," she said, tearfully, "was everything we had."

When Hurricane Fran arrived in Ohio, she was nothing more than a rain storm. She had given the heart of Carolina a beating and a couple of visitors much to contemplate. Believe me, it didn't have a thing to do with the fall window washing we'd left behind.

We traveled home from the South the same way we'd gone down. Meandering. Going back, our minds were full of new things to ponder. How fragile life is. How little control we have over it all, and the important lesson of putting life's particulars into perspective. Material things can be replaced. A daughter, a son-in-law, and two precious children cannot.

Marrying Off the Baby

Several years back we had two weddings. Our oldest daughter married in June that year, our middle daughter in October. Our middle daughter said all she wanted was a new car. Her father helped her get one. Money exchanged hands. Next thing we knew, she wanted a husband too. You cannot trust daughters.

After that busy year, I figured when the time came for our youngest daughter to get married the wedding would be a snap. Not. It seems having two weddings in one year is a walk in the park compared to marrying off the baby. It wasn't just that the price of weddings had skyrocketed. Marrying off the baby was significantly different from marrying off a regular daughter.

This is the wedding of the one in whose presence the word no has never been uttered. She's had the best her family could afford. No. She's had better, and, as with many last borns, our youngest offspring had perfected the art of sweet talking.

By the time this one was ready for her trousseau, we were old. Tired. Worn down. Besides, she had two older sisters standing in the wings to pick up anything the old people voted down. This girl always had her heart's desire.

Her every whim. She was, after all, cute. Eyes of blue. Hair of gold and she was the baby.

Just try reining in the baby when shopping for the wedding gown. The dress in which she would present herself to her young groom was dress number 3000 to be marched into the dressing room at the eighth bridal boutique. The heap in the chair was the mother-of-the-bride, propped up by the matron-of-honor who had already turned stony-eyed, but that dress! Ah, the dress. It had billions of tiny seed pearls and sequins and a train that went to Chicago and back. What a find. Our baby whirled and twirled. She preened in front of those mirrors. Why, the dress was a buy at any cost!

Now, finding just the right veil to go with this ensemble wouldn't be easy. It couldn't be too frothy. Yet it had to be frothy enough. There would be no stinting on the shopping for The Veil. Even though it was but a simple bit of tulle, it would rest on top of the bride's head like a halo, propelling her down the aisle. Veil shopping went on for many weeks. Finally, the ultimate veil artisan was located, thankfully within the state, and she was fitted with The Veil.

Next, came the choosing of the wedding cake. At the cake shoppe we were ushered into an elegant room where the table was set with lace and flowers and where wedding cakes clearly reigned. Cakes with flowers. Cakes with pearls. Cakes with cherubs. We sipped coffee and sampled. There was cake laced with raspberries, lemons, almonds, fudge. There were any number of variations. All lip smacking good. "How can you count cost," the father-of-the-bride whispered, "when it comes to the wedding cake? I'll take another piece of almond, thank you." The baby said it had to be many tiered. Lighted. With fountains and ribboned pillars and pearls. It would taste delectable, and look spectacular. On top of this exquisite confection would perch a bouquet of fresh roses, and our baby's cake would be the centerpiece of the celebration.

Then, there was the photographer who would record this glorious event, this wedding of our last born. The bride and groom would pose in the church. In the garden. In the reception hall. In front of a backdrop. With all the attendants. The parents. Grandparents. Alone. Together. With friends. With the flowers. Without the flowers.

Speaking of flowers. Did I say plenty? Make that plenty, plenty. Roses. Gardenias. Lilies, and Baby's Breath. Loads of Baby's Breath. Flowing from the pews would be yards of white frothy netting caught in huge bows. Did I mention centerpieces? Candles?

What about the reception? Say good bye to the V.F.W. hall, the Moose Lodge, the Eagles club. It was on to the local jockey club. The friends and relatives of our baby must dine in style.

They came from Pittsburgh. St. Clair Shores. Baltimore and Raleigh. There was the clan from Cleveland who cleaned up everything from the chicken to the quiche to the tortellini.

It was a lovely wedding. We have the photographs to prove it.

However, as committed and in love as those two were that day, the union didn't last.

Their parting gift to each other and to their families was a set of triplets. Three little ones to love. Two boys and a girl. When the door closed on their marriage, one opened with another chapter yet to be written.

Barbara A. Whittington

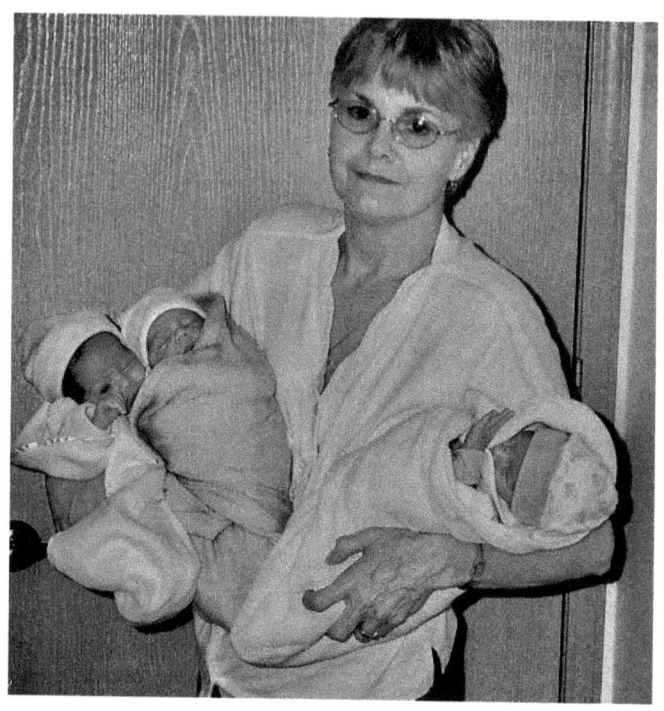

Newborn Triplets and Nana Barb

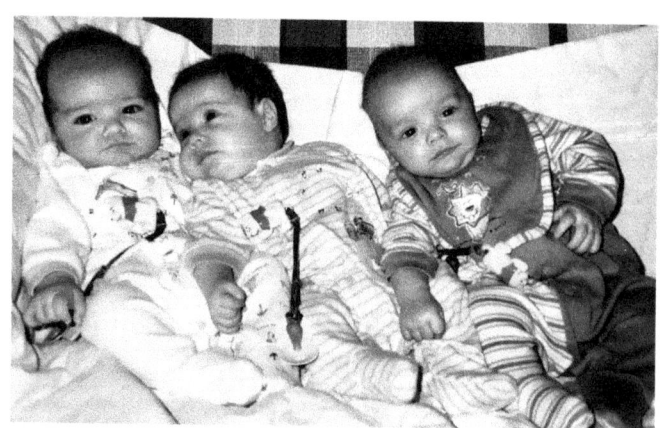

Grandma's Rocking Chair

Grandma's rocking chair -
Headed for Wisconsin
Loaded in a U-Haul, nestled
Between an antique secretary,
And a refinished dresser -
Mirror long gone.
Passed on to our daughter.
Our three year-old triplet
Grandchildren, faces pressed
To the window of the van,
Wave good bye to Nana and Papa
In the driveway-their tears
Breaking our hearts.
Our daughter, Jill,
Heavy with the child of her new spouse,
Hums to the children
And soon they are fast asleep.
The rocking will start
While baby is in the womb,
This new grandson of ours,
Whose name before
He's even born is Austin Cole.
He will learn from his mother
How rocking soothes the soul.
Nourishes the spirit.
Links us one to the other
And to generations past and future.
Just as we were linked
As children forming the circle
For ring around the rosey.

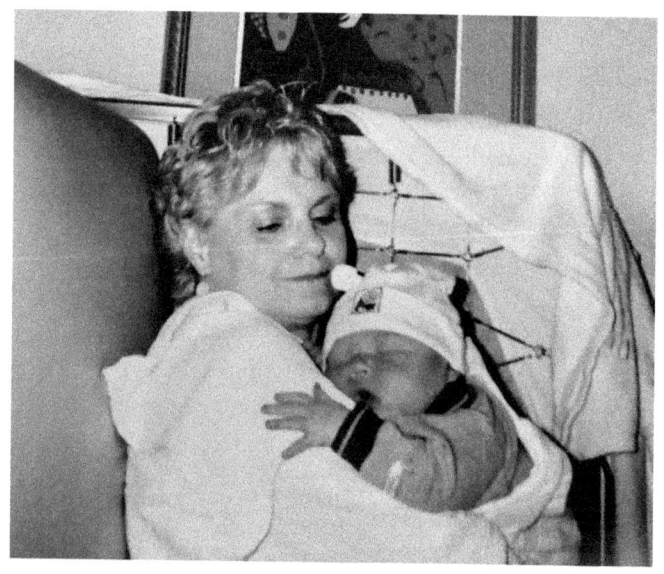

Austin Cole, our last grandchild, with his Nana

Imperfect Family Makes the Holiday

Glancing at the newspaper early Thanksgiving morning, I saw a picture of the perfect family getting ready to enjoy their holiday dinner.

At the head of the table sat father, in a fashionable three-piece suit, skillfully carving the big bird. Mother, elegant in silk and jewels, sat beside him and cradled a smiling infant. Two exquisitely groomed children were looking with adoration at their parents.

In matching cashmere sweaters, aunt and uncle held hands as though they were ready to start the prayer chain. Grandmother and grandfather, a handsome couple in designer knits, had their arms around the youngsters in a warm embrace.

At my house, an all-out search was on for "the tablecloth." I knew we had one. We'd used it the year before, or the year before that. On the kitchen counter sat a partially thawed thirty-pound bird waiting to be stuffed.

The pumpkin pies baked the night before were already weeping. The kids, having just recuperated from the flu, were playing Pilgrims and Indians in wrinkled pajamas, paper collars, and feathered hats.

My sister, who was supposed to come and help, had just phoned to say her flight had been delayed. Right then, I wished I was in Virginia Beach, too. The rest of the family was conveniently snowed in at a Holiday Inn somewhere on the turnpike.

When my husband rounded up all the guys from the neighborhood and turned on the television for the pre-game warm-up, I sensed a migraine coming on.

Finally, we sat down to eat our holiday feast. My husband was at the head of the table, just like in the picture, except he was dressed in his favorite orange and brown sweatshirt. He was using my new electric knife to make mincemeat out of the bird.

I sat beside him, in denim not silk, and tried to cradle our squirming infant. Silently perched on the edge of their chairs, the two older kids were shooting hostile looks at their father. It made no difference that he'd apologized for running over their bikes in the driveway. They hold grudges.

They did ask for seconds, though, and to their brief prayer they'd added, "Since we don't have bikes, please, let it snow so we can use our sleds."

Later that night, I collapsed in a chair to read the article that went with the picture of "the perfect family." As it turned out, it wasn't a family at all. The people were members of a struggling theatrical group, giving their first performance.

I looked at the snapshot we'd taken that day. Our table was laden with good things to eat. The camera had caught a winning smile from the baby. Even the kids looked somewhat happy.

Was it the fresh snow or the gifts from the relatives? Yes, they came, and though they were late, they brought along enough happiness to make further explanations unnecessary.

Holidays aren't perfect. Neither are families. They're unique. Special. This year I intend to enjoy both.

Thanksgiving Poem

8000 Calorie Poem

May your stuffing be tasty,
May your turkey plump,
May your potatoes and gravy
Have not a lump
May your yams be delicious
And your pies take the prize,
And may your Thanksgiving dinner
Stay off your thighs!

The Gift of Time

As Mother's Day approaches and advertisements for flowers, cards, and candy adorn the shop windows, I wonder how many mothers would exchange a store-bought gift for a few hours of the giver's time. Not time sliced thin and pressed between obligations but time freely given without the hands of a clock to interrupt.

Giving gifts is, indeed, a way of expressing feelings. If time has been spent developing a loving relationship, it will continue to grow after the flowers have withered, the cards have been put away, and the candy has disappeared.

Listen to a mother and travel into her world through her eyes. One short trip with her can reveal why she is who she is today. Patience and understanding can close the gap of many years.

Every Mother's Day, my friend spends the day with her elderly mother. She hears the same stories over, stories she can repeat backwards. She listens intently to every word, though. She believes no one can tell the stories quite as well.

The special look on her mother's face is the irreplaceable gift my friend receives.

Talking and sharing ideas can bring different lifestyles in touch. Duplicating a lifestyle isn't necessary, but communication is. Triumphs are doubled, and failures are halved when shared in the embrace of a mother.

Sometimes a helping hand will make a Mother's Day more pleasant for some mothers. Lifting a pair of heavy drapes to a window that her hands can't reach, or doing a chore that she can't manage is appreciated long afterward.

Time spent with a mother doing anything is time well spent. I know. My mother doesn't want more cologne or another nightgown. She cherishes my time. Driving her to visit an old friend, or out into the country where she grew up, or to the church where she can no longer walk is my way of saying I care.

I try to give her what she gives me: love, unmonitored by the hands of a clock.

On Time

My elderly friend
has
nothing
but endless hours
to fill.
I have
husband,
kids,
dog,
and dentist,
wanting to be
waited on,
fed,
petted
and paid.
Time plays tricks,
giving less,
early
and more
too late.

For Mary Schumaker who, with her husband Walter, ran the mini mart and gas station in our neighborhood in Chesterland. Mary had hours to fill and I had little time to visit when I stopped for bread. Now, like Mary, I have hours to fill. Finally, I understand. Mary appreciated a friendly face and a little chat. Rest in peace Mary and Walter.

Spring Cleaning - Mother's Way

Springtime! I catch the faint smell of lilies-of-the-valley, feel the warm breeze from the open window, hear the schoolchildren clamoring with excitement as they get off the bus at the corner and I am transported back to those first warm days of spring when I was a kid.

Peeling off hot dusty socks and wading in the creek at the back of our house was one of the highlights of my day. I was as much at home there as the frogs and tadpoles. Another favorite pastime was taking a lunch and going up the steep, honeysuckle-covered hillside to visit the old cemetery. All afternoon I'd munch peanut butter sandwiches and read the inscriptions on the ancient tombstones. As the shadows lengthened and darkness threatened, I'd head for home with every ghost imaginable nipping at my heels.

Only one thing marred my zest for springtime. I'd come home on one of those sultry days, tired and spent from my expeditions, to find mother putting the wood-framed wire screens in the windows. That one task signaled the beginning of the thing I most dreaded, mother's yearly campaign against dirt. Spring cleaning.

The first thing to be hit was the bedrooms. Out into the yard went every movable object. There was no such thing as a bed too big or a doorway too small. Standing in the empty rooms and staring out the window at the beds on the back lawn seemed strange, but, no time for dawdling, I was told. On to the chores at hand. Mattresses were aired. Bed slats were scrubbed. Headboards, dressers and chests were varnished. Heavy rugs were slung over the clothesline and beaten with a broom. Mother could spot a speck of dirt a mile away. I know. I was offered her glasses more than once.

From ceiling to floor, the kitchen walls were washed with pine cleaner. Wearing rubber gloves, mother would clean the oven, removing my unsuccessful attempts at baking for the 4-H Club. The refrigerator and freezer, no matter how full, were unloaded and washed. What could a box of soda do on a shelf, she wanted to know? It had to be mixed with a little water and elbow grease to do the job right.

Baseboards were my specialty. Mother saw to it that the loudest complainer got that job. Oh, the spiders and cobwebs down on that floor! Fearing for my life as baseboard washer, I finished the job in record time. I usually earned the right to do it over. That time, I got the corners.

Because the floors were last didn't mean they got any less attention. Mother cleaned with concentration, demolishing every dust ball that got in her way. She required more buckets and rags than a leaky gymnasium. After the floors were waxed, I was encouraged to buff them. It didn't take much to entice me onto the floor with my white bobby socks.

Finally, the furniture was back in place and crisp sheets, smelling of sunshine, were on the beds. Out under the large willow tree in the backyard I could rest with a tall glass of iced tea and daydream about the lazy summer months ahead.

Only mother had work yet to do. It was time for the finishing touches. Armed with her imagination, a wringer washer, and a box of RIT dye, she set to work. She believed in experimenting and experiment she did! With one box of that color she performed magic. Anything washable got dipped into her potion. One year we had purple bedspreads and pale purple curtains. The house was not only clean, it was coordinated.

Each year I give much thought to spring cleaning mother's way. I wander from room to room, making several lists. Somehow, I lack her enthusiasm, her originality. The process she went through wasn't just cleaning to her. It was the rejuvenation of her own spirit, a spirit grown tired after a long, dull winter.

My own self-cleaning appliances and electric gadgets accomplish a great deal of work every day. It just isn't the same. Out on the patio, I sip iced tea and watch a squirrel scamper up a tree. The furniture doesn't need painting. The bedspreads are still bright and colorful. Besides, I don't have a wringer washer. However, I do have some peanut butter for sandwiches and a long, leisure day ahead.

I hope the honeysuckle is still in bloom at the old cemetery and frogs and tadpoles still abound in the little creek.

Barbara's Fruit n Nut Scones

Bake at 375°

2 cups all-purpose flour
2 teaspoons baking powder
1/2 teaspoon baking soda
1/4 teaspoon salt
1/2 cup butter
1   8 ounce carton dairy sour cream
1 large egg
1/2 cup granulated sugar plus sugar to sprinkle on before baking.
2/3 cup snipped dried apricots
1/2 cup citrus zest (Orange and or Lemon)
1/2 cup powdered sugar
A few drops citrus juice or flavoring for glaze. Add milk to glaze consistency.
1/2 cup chopped toasted walnuts or pecans

Preheat oven to 375°F. Lightly grease a large baking sheet or line a baking sheet with parchment paper; set aside. In bowl stir together flour, baking powder, soda, and salt. Cut in butter to resemble coarse crumbs; set aside. In a bowl stir together sour cream, egg, granulated sugar, and zest; add to flour mixture. Combine just until moistened. Stir in apricots and nuts. Roll into circle on floured board, thickness should be thicker than pie crust. I make two circles. Cut in wedges. Sprinkle with sugar. Bake 12 to 15 minutes or until golden and toothpick inserted in center comes out clean. Cool on rack. For glaze, stir together powdered sugar and flavoring. Enough milk to make a glaze, drizzle over scones. (Tip- because I love citrus I save all lemon and orange peels and freeze. Then I use the food processor to make zest for baking) Makes 18- 20 scones.

Like My Mother

I never wanted to be like my mother. Growing up, I thought she was old fashioned and too old to know what was going on in the world. Certainly she was too old to know what was going on in my life. Back then, the very last thing I wanted to be was like mother.

Today as I go about my routine, it hit me. I'm exactly like my mother. She started her day with coffee. I do too. I eat a banana and yogurt. She often ate toast. No real breakfast for us, although she often made a big breakfast for everyone else. Biscuits, eggs, sausage and gravy.

Each day, I make my bed and straighten the house as if I'm expecting visitors. She did the same.

Every morning, just like mother, I watch the news to get the latest of the good and the bad in the world.

I can't relax until every chore is finished. Mother couldn't either. If I'm sitting, I will fold clothes or make lists. I also journal. Mother didn't enjoy writing. She did make lists though. Some of her time was spent mending and ironing clothes. She made a few quilts on her treadle sewing machine. She called them rough but I called them beautiful. Her hands were always busy. Either deep in biscuit dough, pie crust, or washing dishes, she didn't believe in idle hands.

She was a hard worker, physically. I believe she could have dug a ditch if necessary. For me hard work is washing floors or cleaning windows.

My mother and I are different in one area. She loved to garden and work in the yard, cleaning, picking up sticks, planting flowers, carrying rail road ties one year with my step father to make a border for her flower bed. She'd rather work than to do anything. She planted, weeded, and loved on her garden. She canned and preserved all her life.

I've never planted even one plant. I did hire some neighboring Amish boys to plant flowers one year when we lived in the country. They said they'd never planted flowers as that was a job for the girls in the family. They explained the process as they knew it. Dig a hole, pour in water, add the plant, cover the hole, and water again. I agreed that was the process of planting from having watched my mother.

Mother simply enjoyed being outdoors. Working. I enjoyed the outdoors too. Sitting. Reading a good book in one of the porch rockers, or sitting on the back deck in the evening and watching wild life skitter past from the hay field beyond. Often I saw a pair of deer leaping across the fields. I call that loving the outdoors, my way.

All of her 87 years, mother was devoted to her family. My wish is that I can be a fraction of the woman she was.

I'm sitting here remembering all the good things about my mom. How much fun we had together, talking, laughing, loving. I'm hoping my children will remember some good things about me. Who knows? Maybe they'll turn out to be just a little like me.

Life has a way of playing tricks on us. It often gives us what we least desire, yet it ends up being exactly what we need.

Mother and Ralph taken after Ralph told her he had joined the Army. Around 1944. She was not a happy mother.

Barbara A. Whittington

Mother, in her new dress and jacket, for a trip to Olin Mills Studio, arranged by her daughters. An unnecessary trip, she said, as she wasn't a fan of having her photo taken.

Mother and Me

I'm beginning to see
My mother in me.
Can it be
That I am she?
Her words echo in my head,
"Don't do as I do,
Do as I said!"
I see her face
In my mirror
I open my mouth
And I can hear her.
I am she and she is me
And that's as fine
As I'll ever be.
Now grown gray
With much to say.
So, wish me well
And don't you tell!
I'm beginning to see
My Mother in me.

Barbara A. Whittington

Mother and Me

A Special Woman a Special Time

A few days before Christmas, I talked with a woman I've known all my life. She's 75 but has the spirit of a child. When my long-distance call reached her, she was sitting in her living room admiring her Christmas tree.

Now that her children are grown, she decorates a two-foot-tall artificial tree. "Who on earth would pay the price for a real one?" she wanted to know.

"Ah," she continued, "you should see the packages under this tree." I knew she had already unwrapped half of them. She never would put off until tomorrow what she could do today. Oh, the presents had been rewrapped ever so carefully. On Christmas morning she would repeat the ritual with renewed interest.

That day we talked of holidays, weather, family, mutual friends. After our conversation, I sat down with my coffee to think about this woman.

Her life has been one of challenge. When she was 33, she witnessed the death of her 10-month old son. "He was a blue baby," she told me once at the cemetery. "He had a hole in his heart. If only the doctors had had more medical knowledge back then. They didn't. You never get over losing a baby," she sighed.

I remember the chubby, brown-eyed baby from the small oval picture on his marble tombstone.

At the age of 42, she lost her husband. She reassembled her life and finished raising her children by working nights cleaning offices in a factory.

Two major surgeries in middle age didn't slow her pace. She continued to work. She was born with a purpose to her life; not just to survive but to enjoy the survival.

At 69, she was still going strong, cooking, cleaning, scrubbing her porches daily, and gardening. When she started having pain in her left leg, she told me repeatedly, "The doctor says it's just arthritis."

She took aspirin and prescribed medications. She tried home remedies, putting the aspirins in the liniment she rubbed on her leg. "It didn't work," she said, smiling, as the pain continued to increase.

When she was 72, she went to a new doctor. He found a cancerous tumor. It had deteriorated the large bone in her leg. She underwent tests to determine whether cancer was anywhere else. After a bone marrow test, I asked if it was painful. She answered tartly, "It's like having a knife stuck in your tail bone."

When the doctor decided to amputate her leg, I was scared. Before the surgery, her family and friends were with her. "I'd go in your place if I could," I said, helplessly. "Look at you," she scolded. "You're not as strong as I am."

As she was wheeled down the hall, I heard her tell a tearful young nurse, "Don't worry, honey, I'll be all right."

She came home from the hospital for one day. She went back with a blood clot in her left lung. The oxygen and shots in her stomach to dissolve the clot were just procedures to her.

Six months later, she was walking on an artificial limb. "Don't try to bury me until I'm dead," she kept saying when she sensed any opposition to her independence.

That summer she planted and harvested her yearly garden. She went back to porch scrubbing, too.

I tried not to nag. On my visits, I could bring home evidence of her health in the form of green beans and grape jelly. It was good to see flowers blooming in the boxes on her front porch.

Last year, I noticed a lump on her right leg. "Yes," she finally admitted, "my leg is sore." Her doctor confirmed another tumor. Because it was caught in time, it could be treated.

For 11 days, she traveled to the hospital for radiation. She was installed in a tiny room, told not to move or sneeze (cough, scratch or anything else) and was left alone with her thoughts. Anything could be endured for a precious limb, for independence.

That day as I sat remembering, letting my coffee grow cold, I was warmed. I could hear her as she opened those gifts, exclaiming over the beauty and extravagance of the smallest one.

My gifts will never be enough to match what she has given me through the years. She's such a special person, and not just because she's my mother.

When mother read this essay, she said it made her cry. "I didn't mean to make you sad." She said, "I wasn't sad. It made me cry because of how much you care about me."

Christmas in the 50's. Mother, Sue and **me**. Mother always made our Christmas special with her Coconut Christmas Cake, fresh fruit salad, and her popular homemade dressing that I still cannot duplicate.

A Lonely Christmas

A large statue of the Virgin Mary guards the entrance to St. Francis Hospital. Nearby stands a big, snow-covered pine tree bathed in blue lights. As I pass through the reception area, a life-size, mechanical Santa waves a cheery hello.

On the third floor, under an antiseptic sheet, mother's form looks slight, fragile. I am glad I've come. We kiss and hug and cry. She fusses. I shouldn't have driven so far. The weather is so unpredictable this time of year. The roads are unsafe for a woman alone. Her eyes light up as we talk.

The food is tasteless, she jokes. The trays look suspiciously like the ones she sent back to the kitchen during her last stay two months ago.

Was our respite so short, I wonder?

As we chat, we drink cider from the container on her window sill and munch grapes from the fruit basket on her night stand. The doctors and nurses are good people, she says, but they're just too busy taking care of the patients who're really sick. Besides, she is going to be all right. She says.

The heparin injected in the plug in her arm every four hours does seem to be clearing her lungs of the blood clots faster than the shots she had in her stomach last time. Her chest x-rays have improved. If only she weren't so pale and thin.

Mother says she feels fortunate. Her roommate just came back from surgery. Breast cancer. So, mother, with only one leg and blood clots in her lungs, cares for their needs using the bedside buzzer.

From the intercom in the hall strains of "Rudolph, the Red-Nosed Reindeer," drift into the small room at the end of the long corridor. It doesn't matter that the television doesn't work.

There's enough activity, mother says, outside her doorway. We watch as the head nurse makes her rounds with the medicine cart. She pauses only briefly to direct an elderly man back to his room.

Last Christmas, mother enjoyed a healthy reprieve. No hospitals, no tumors, no radiation. This year, well, mother says a hospital is a lonely place at Christmas. From the third floor window, I look down on the dark, deserted city street below. The other visitors have all gone home, past the mechanical Santa, the blue-lit Christmas tree and the Virgin Mary, who on this night will have my help watching over her flock.

Christmas 1950s. Me, Brownie, Mother

The Red Christmas Cane

I was walking around on an old cane that year
Grumping and complaining that the holidays were here.
I looked out my window and as far as I could see
There were lights, stars, and angels adorning every tree.
And I might as well tell you, it bugged the heck out of me!
If I hadn't fallen and an ankle broken
I'd be out at the mall buying holiday tokens.
A scarf for the mail man, a tie for my son,
A big can of tuna for my old cat Bun.
Instead, I was stuck in the house that year
And didn't expect Christmas to make its way here.
I sat in my rocker and let the tears fly
Thinking that the season was passing me by.
THEN I saw Mr. Mackey in his big front window
Holding a sign that said, "Happy Holiday, Belinda."
Mr. Mackey, you see, was a wheelchair bound man
But, still, there he was, a greeting in his hand.
A smile was on this kind man's face
Though he was confined in a heavy back brace.
Well, I looked up his number and I called Mr. Mackey
Hoping what I had to say wasn't WAY too tacky.
"Mr. Mackey," I said, "Please share my Christmas cake."
Since he lived alone, I was sure he didn't bake.
"Why, Belinda, my dear, all this time I've been waiting
To make sure some other fellow you were not dating.
"Come for a party and bring what you might,
A holiday fire together we will light."
So, I set out later on my red Christmas cane
For Charlie Mackey's house just across the lane.
And by spring, Charlie asked me to be his bride -
When I said yes, we both sat down and cried.
Though my red Christmas cane has been put away
Charlie Mackey and I celebrate Christmas every day.

A New Year's Greeting - with apologies to Dr. Seuss

Cleaning up after the holiday
Isn't quite as much fun,
As on the day
When the decorations were strung.
There was my family, all spruced, in the den,
With an eggnog toast, and a cheer, "Let's begin."
We set about bedecking every pillar and post,
Window and mantle -
With ribbon, wreath, Santa, and candle.
By the end of the evening
The tree was aglitter.
The windows were glowing
With the candlesticks flicker.
The children were happy
Mom and Pop, too.
To think we did all this.
You, you and you!
But, then, the week after
Rolled quickly 'round.
No time to un-trim.
We headed to town.
To return all our presents.
To see a quick show.
What? It's the middle of January
The trimming must go.
Undo each ribbon. Undo each bow.
Untie the wreaths
Get that tree in tow.
It's out to the trash bin
Arms loaded, we go.
Away go the boxes.
The cards and the letters.

Barbara A. Whittington

Out comes our list of "Things to do better."
Resolutions. Affirmations.
Declarations. Proclamations.
Where's that old diet?
By Jiminy, we'll try it!
It's a New Year we're facing and face it we will.
Without eggnog or fudge or even a pill.
We'll face it together -
Oh, taste buds be still!
Until, oh no, here comes the BILL.
Or, as in our case, it's many -
Giving the post man exercise aplenty.
At my house we're still undoing the fun
Dusting and washing and rising and wiping
Trinkets and dishes and goblets, and griping,
"Next year, it's a vacation we'll take.
By Amtrak or horseback or roller skate!"
Who cares how we do it, we plan and we plot.
Next year it's to the tropics.
Anywhere that it's HOT.
Whatever we do, one thing is clear.
We're wishing you and yours a
VERY HAPPY NEW YEAR

Lisa's Christmas, before she had siblings.

Rakes and Flowers and Memories

When I was a kid, the Saturday before Memorial or Decoration Day, as we called it, was always reserved for going to the Walker Chapel cemetery in the country. Grandma would be up at dawn and waiting for us on her front porch in Hometown. By the time mother's Dodge Dart rounded the street corner in a cloud of dust, my grandmother would be out the gate, smoothing her crisp, cotton house dress and adjusting her starched sunbonnet. Her thick heeled shoes were no-nonsense, her stockings sturdy. Though she was thin, there was nothing sheer about Grandma.

Red geraniums, white peonies, and purple pansies spilled from the large wooden basket on Grandma's arm. She'd stow the basket and a variety of rakes and gardening tools in the car trunk before climbing into the front seat beside mother.

I didn't know, then, about measuring love with rakes and flowers but Grandma did.

As the car snaked its way along winding country roads, the somber mood in the front seat failed to inhibit my behavior. Hanging out the back window, with the wind rushing in my face, I'd laugh with delight and grab at the sweet smelling honeysuckle slapping the sides of the car. The world was mine: the tall white farmhouses, the lush green fields, the blue sky overhead.

Eventually, I would settle down, push myself primly into a corner of the back seat and breathe deeply the scent of fried chicken drifting up from the trunk. Occasionally, I'd look out the window to see a farmer with a horse-drawn plow cutting furrows in the reddish brown earth along Eighteen Mile Creek Road.

Finally, we'd arrive at the church, Walker Chapel, in Given. I'd hop from the car, full of anticipation, and then stop, overwhelmed by the sight before me.

Tombstones covered the hillside as far as my eyes could see. Some of the stones were marble, huge and ornately carved. Others were small and simple. A few had been hand-hewn so long ago the engravings had eroded back into the rock.

"It's too bad," mother said, shaking her head, "that even in death, money sets people apart."

The old metal money box was still there on the fence, securely fastened with a piece of wire. Coins rattled as we pushed open the gate.

"That box," Grandma said, making her way across the grassy slope, "is to remind folks who come to visit but never to mow or clean that a cemetery has to be kept up. Besides," she'd nod to me, "the man who mows has to eat."

When my eyes found our family plots across the grassy knoll, I didn't have to count. I could tell by looking, all our graves were still there.

While the grown-ups unloaded the car, I hurried over to the little white church with the steeple. I'd stand on tiptoe at one of the windows and peer inside. I liked the purple attendance banner with the gold lettering that hung near the altar. Black hymnals were neatly lined in racks at the back of each polished pew. The church was ready for the service the next day.

Behind the church, I'd sit at the weathered picnic table swinging my legs and watching black and white cows graze in a neighboring field. "There's work to be done," Grandma's voice would ring out and I'd drag myself reluctantly back to the cemetery.

The caretaker had already been there with his mowing machine. Great sweeping paths had been made around the hillside. Yellowed bits of newspaper and debris had blown in from the roadway below and wedged against the tombstones. Weeds still stood tall in every corner.

While Grandma raked, I carried baskets of twigs and leaves and dumped them into a rusty barrel by the fence. Sometimes a strong wind would swirl around us and the leaves would blow away faster than I could scoop them into my basket. Grandma's sunbonnet would fly off her head and tumble, pell-mell, down the hillside. Chasing it over a grassy mound, I'd capture it in a fence corner.

"You're going to wake the dead!" My three aunts, Lucy, Gay, and Wanda, who had joined us would cry in unison at my whoop of joy at the capture of Grandma's bonnet. My aunts brought their own rakes, their own flowers, and their own ideas. If I played even one game of "hop over the grave," they'd squeal, "You are standing on Poppy. Get off him, right now. You hear, Bobbie Ann?"

Meanwhile mother would be planting flowers, patting rich, black dirt around each one, and watering them from the Mason jar she'd brought from home. No matter how many flowers she put on a grave, Grandma always added another. There was no such thing as "over decorating."

In between my twig carrying, bonnet chasing, and aunt dodging, I'd pause frequently to study two graves. They were the ones I got to put fancy floral wreaths on. Relationships were written on satin ribbon. FATHER. BROTHER. Mother became unusually busy during the time I arranged the wreaths on those graves. My daddy, who died when I was two, got the biggest wreath with the red ribbon. My baby brother, who died before I was born, got the wreath with the blue bow.

From his oval photo on the tombstone, our baby watched with dark solemn eyes as I placed the tiny wreath on his grave.

At last, Grandma put down her rake and wiped her brow. Mother would walk down by the fence near the road. Her hands shaded her eyes as she looked back up at us. Finally, she waved. Grandma smiled. Our decorations could be seen by everyone who traveled the little country road.

After loading the tools into the car, the adults slipped some folded bills through the slot in the metal money box, and carried the picnic boxes to the table under the shade tree. There, the conversation took on contest form. Whose fried chicken was the crispiest? Whose pie crust the flakiest? Grandma's blue eyes twinkled as she winked at me. We both knew. Every morsel was equally delicious.

On the way home, I slept, my head resting in Grandma's lap.

Now that I've grown up and moved away from Putnam County, West Virginia, there is no set time to go back to clean and decorate the cemetery. Vacations don't always coincide with Memorial Day, or the Saturday before, but, when I do go back, I take rakes and flowers. Flowers for Grandma and Mother, and now for my sweet sister, Donna Sue.

Walker Chapel Church

December 7, 1941
The Memories Sear - The Blame Washes Away

"War! Oahu Bombed By Japanese Planes." Many summers ago at Pearl Harbor, I read the shocking headlines from a copy of the Honolulu Star-Bulletin, dated Sunday, December 7, 1941. I was waiting in line to board a tour boat to go to the USS Arizona Memorial. Finally, moving toward an empty boat, I noted that most of the people on the crowded platform were Japanese.

On the short ride across the harbor, I listened to a guide describe the events of that fateful day. As the boat approached the white concrete building, the guide concluded, "The battleship Arizona still rests at the bottom of the harbor in 38 feet of water just eight feet below the water's surface. The memorial is an enclosed bridge that spans the sunken hull, but touches no part of the ship itself. Oil will continue to seep from the battleship for many years."

When I stepped off the tour boat, I saw the American flag flying over a small part of the ship that is visible above the water.

Inside the memorial, I was swept back to the day of the disastrous bombing. From the walls, pictures of the battleship in flames and sinking, looked down at me and seared themselves on my mind. I couldn't appreciate the mementos salvaged from the ship knowing that 1,177 men were entombed below in the battleship's blasted hulk.

A loudspeaker was effectively re-creating the day with the sound of bombs exploding and chaotic outcries.

As I stared out an opening in the wall at the calm blue water, I was lost in thought for a few minutes. Then black oil gurgled to the water's surface. Though the temperature was 85, I turned away, chilled.

From the middle of the memorial, I could see the ship through a glass covered opening in the floor. I thought of the many men and all the ambitions and dreams that had gone down with the ship. I thought of the mothers, fathers, spouses, and children, who had been left behind with the burden of unanswered questions.

I wondered how the men would feel if they knew the memorial was filled with Japanese tourists. Silently, I suffered their indignation.

In the shrine room, where the names of the dead men are engraved on a marble wall, I stood in reverence, trying to wish away the horrors of the war.

Nearby, a Japanese gentleman, left his group and gravely studied the wall. Over the speaker, the names of the men were slowly being read. Ceremoniously, the Japanese man removed an orchid lei from his neck and placed it next to several wreaths on a marble platform. He backed away and was lost in the crowd.

Aboard the tour boat for the return trip, I tried to sort out my emotions. Before my visit, I'd thought of the memorial at Pearl Harbor as another tourist attraction. I'd been tremendously touched by the harsh realities of war and by the wasted lives and destruction.

Why, then, did I feel the need to condemn? Could I blame the Japanese man who had humbly offered the lei? The Japanese couple who sat on the boat in front of me? The somber young Japanese woman on my right? With tears in my eyes, I realized I couldn't blame anyone. I remembered Hiroshima.

Dr. Oz is in My Purse

My husband and I are becoming addicted to the Dr. Oz show. Well, I'm addicted. He just watches and naps during the show. I'm energized by Oz's vim and vigor. He jumps onto stage and within minutes is giving me ways to live longer and better. I find myself jumping up and down with him at the very thought of living long and feeling good.

What's not to like about a man named Mehmet who comes on and cheers me while I eat my steel cut oats, walnuts, and blueberries?

But, let me warn you, if you haven't watched his show, it involves diseased body parts and slabs of body fat brought out on trays to show us what our insides look like on a bad day.

Everything he talks about, whether it's a sex dysfunction, sleep, or daily living, there is something that can be bought at the pharmacy or health food store to alleviate the problem. From erectile dysfunction to constipation, Dr. Oz is all over it.

Some of the stuff he recommends can even be plucked out of the yard. Take sassafras root for example. When I learned one of the trees in our yard was sassafras, I was out there on my knees paying homage to the tree and instructing my husband on how to cut one of its roots so we could enjoy a cup of healthy tea. After several hours of major chopping on his part with his trusty dull ax, we ended up with a handful of roots. I cleaned and boiled the roots that very afternoon. The tea was quite tasty though now I can't remember what it was good for.

Many feel Dr. Oz's word is gospel. I buy every pill, vitamin, and herb he suggests. I had to rearrange the kitchen cupboard to make room for all my new acquisitions. I've added a number of spices and herbs to my collection, including curry, fennel, sesame, and turmeric.

My husband says after I take all this stuff, I'll either be bionic or dead. I'm not sure which he's rooting for. Somehow it seems he isn't with me on this.

Dr. Oz and I were clipping along and getting to know each other rather well when I discovered he was getting into my purse. More specifically, my wallet.

All of his recommendations were costing me a pretty penny. Many pretty pennies it turned out. I knew I had to put a stop to our relationship but I was dreading it. However, it was taken out of my hands. It was cold turkey for us. Our satellite went out and we were notified there was a major glitch to restoring it to our area. That's one of the joys of living in the country.

However, this time rather than costing me more money, this break in satellite service was saving me some pretty pennies. Many pennies. Sayonara, Dr. Oz. Here's hoping the break will be long enough to end my addiction.

The Little Guy

Lately, I've felt as though I'm maneuvering the rapids of the New River. In reality, I'm traveling the maze of my husband's health care issues and trying to build a bridge between our medical coverage and our medical bills.

My husband was a salaried worker for General Motors for 27 years. Most of his years were spent in Cleveland at the Coit Road plant where he worked in security. His job came with much responsibility, a good salary and the promise of a decent retirement. He was one of the last employees to work at the Coit Road facility, helping to shut down the plant he had come to love after all the years he spent there. His schedule was seven days on and one day off for years.

After the plant closed, he was transferred to GM's Hamilton plant in Cincinnati for a three month stint.

The next job opening was in Detroit. After a few months of working in Michigan, he was transferred to Fisher Guide in Columbus. It was a welcome move that put us closer to elderly parents in West Virginia.

My husband was dedicated to GM, not only as an employee, but as a consumer, buying only GM cars for 30 years and encouraging our three daughters to do the same.

The only benefit from GM that my husband has left is a minimal life insurance policy. Recently, a letter from GM informed him that the company retains the right to cancel that policy. An advisory letter usually arrives ahead of the letter that cuts a benefit.

As the spouse of a GM retiree, I've lost my life insurance and most of my health benefits. The little I have left is costly and comes with a large deductible.

Recently, I mailed a prescription to the GM mail-order pharmacy. Along with the 90-day supply of generic pills came a bill for $227. I learned that GM had combined my prescription coverage with my medical coverage as of January and there was now a deductible of $2,500. The same medication at the local grocery store chain would have cost me just under $100. Same milligrams, same dosage, same 90-day supply.

This isn't about bashing GM. It's about the people who are out of jobs and benefits through no fault of their own. This is about what is happening to the little guy. The guy who worked all his life and depended on his savings, his pension and his Social Security to get him through his golden years.

The little guy doesn't want a second home or a grand vacation. He wants to survive. He wants simple compensation for the years he gave to his company while his hair turned gray and his body grew frail, and the big bucks? They went to the big guys. The upper echelon and that's still where the big bucks are going.

In November 2009, my husband went into what Medicare calls the doughnut hole. Due to his health problems, he had used up his benefits for prescriptions. The two drugs he needed in December cost $500 out of pocket.

Thankfully, we had the $500, but, what about the guy who hasn't got it? We've become judicious in our use of prescription drugs, and we buy from local pharmacies where generics are available.

My husband was hospitalized twice in December. The second time amounted to a two-night, three-day stay. Medicare refused to pay his pharmacy bill -- the medications he takes on a daily basis -- and when I complained to

Medicare, I was told he was an outpatient and that was the reason. A call to the billing department at the hospital assured me that, yes, my husband, who had been hospitalized two nights and three days, was considered an outpatient. It's the terminology, she said. I see it as another way of getting out of paying health benefits.

One would expect that expensive premium health care policies would come with premium health care benefits. Not so.

The bottom line is my husband and I are still making it, but for how long? I don't know, and we're not alone.

Help Me Make it Through a Month

The wind was bitter, cutting right through my wool slacks and fur-lined coat as I made my way through the slushy parking lot and into the warm, brightly lit grocery store.

Glancing at my list, I hurried about picking up lettuce and tomatoes for a salad.

At the meat counter, I paused to mutter briefly over the prices, but I didn't have time to deliberate. I'd left work early because of the icy Cleveland roads and I wanted to beat the rush hour traffic home. I grabbed a package of ground meat and moved on.

As I went up and down the aisles, I kept having to maneuver my cart around an old man who seemed to need an inordinate amount of time to move from one section of the store to the other.

Annoyed at having my traffic pattern interrupted, I stopped and watched the old man. His gait was hampered by a severe limp. An uncooperative shopping cart further impeded his journey.

There was something about the man I couldn't quite put my finger on. Studying him soon became more important than getting home early.

The man seemed preoccupied. At the end of every aisle he stopped to scrutinize and rearrange the items in his cart.

The goods on the shelves held some sort of mysterious attraction. He looked with uncertainty at each prospective purchase. He held the item, passing it from one hand to the other, as though weighing its value against something else only he could see.

More than once he made his way slowly back through the store and returned items to the shelf, a box of cheese crackers, some herb tea, a package of pink mints. If not well balanced, his meals were well thought out.

From the bargain table, he chose several dented cans of pork and beans. To his previous selections, he added a large bag of white rice, some powdered milk, and a package of egg noodles.

At the meat counter, his selections were simple: a package of chicken backs and some soup bones.

It wasn't until we were nearing the checkout counter, and I became aware of the crowd, that I realized it was the first of the month.

The old man had been carefully assembling, to the best of his ability, the food he would eat for the next 30 days. He was buying with all the power of a Social Security check.

As I made my way home, no longer caring about the traffic, I thought about my own shopping trips which are not without consternation.

Escalating prices and the shrinking dollar have made me a more conscientious shopper. The easiest-to-prepare and the most-expensive-to-buy are no longer on my list. Nutrition and economy fight a constant battle.

While I may compare the cost of two brands of orange juice and buy the cheaper one, I still have the power to choose. Unlike the old man, if I run out of bread between shopping trips, I have the luxury of going back for more.

Each time I have to shop for food, I dread it more. No only do I have to deal with the exorbitant prices and wonder how long I can survive the race, but I have to deal with the knowledge that my friend, the old man, can't make it nearly as long as I.

Obama versus McCain

I wish I had a crystal ball. "Who will be our next president?" I'd ask, or better yet, "How's the economy in 2010? What's going on in Iraq? What's the price of oil? Does everyone have health insurance?"

However, I don't have a crystal ball and the upcoming election weighs heavily on my mind. Barack Obama or John McCain?

In 1952, we had a billboard of democratic candidate Adlai Stevenson on our front porch and my mother drove voters to the polls. My step father was a diehard Democrat.

My husband comes from a family of staunch conservatives, Republican or the Grand Old Party, all the way. The two of us discuss politics only occasionally. We both agree, however, that regardless of party affiliations we vote for the person whose values mesh with ours.

Now, for the first time in history a black man is in the race.

I got my first taste of white versus black when I was a kid and traveled through Virginia on a Greyhound. I was hit with restrooms and water fountains labeled COLORED. My childish mind could not comprehend that because one's skin was dark he could not mingle with people who were light-skinned. Did color rub off?

It wasn't long before I learned it had nothing to do with color rubbing off. It had to do with deep rooted prejudices and anger that ran like blood through the veins of many. It had to do with personal bias and lack of education. Fast forward to the 2008 election. We have Obama who's black, a man of talent, charisma, and intelligence. At the age of 47, Barack is the unknown factor in this campaign, and he stands for change.

Across the aisle, we have McCain, age 71, the well-known POW and familiar senator. He's running on experience. Well-loved by many.

We ask ourselves, do we want change? Do we want experience? Do we want more of the same? Do we want youth? Age? Black or white?

The important question is, "Which one can turn our country around?"

Here in Southern Ohio where the local IGA has a hitching post for Amish buggies and tractors hauling hay are as common as cars on the road, I conducted my own unscientific poll.

My new neighbor, Rick, a member of the National Guard, said, when asked what he thought of Obama, "I want change. I'm voting for him. I'm tired of industry leaving this country."

When I asked my old neighbor, PJ, from the city, what she thinks of Obama, she said she doesn't. McCain's her man. She added a few other words I cannot print.

Currently my poll is running neck and neck.

It doesn't take a crystal ball to tell us we're in a mess. We need help. Which candidate is best suited for the job?

I don't know.

Many of us won't make up our minds until election day. Then, it will be years before we know if we made the right decision.

Eyebrows: Help!

Those of you who still have your natural eyebrows, please raise your hands.

Okay, thanks. Now, let's see the hands of those who have eyebrows that are not the greatest but still in place and serving you well. Good! I appreciate.

All those who had your hands in the air are now dismissed. Sorry. The topic we are going to discuss or cuss is the lack of eyebrows. When I was a kid like most of you in the audience, I had normal eyebrows, normal shape, brown in color.

It was in my teens, when I started to pay attention to my eyebrows. It was then they began to let me down. I first learned to pluck and tweeze the hairs above my eyes from watching my sister do hers. She had black brows in a perfect arch over big brown eyes. Sweet.

That wasn't my experience. Far from it. I either took off too many tweezing or too little. I never got the hang of tweezing or plucking. Finally, I gave that up.

For a few years I let my brows grow in a random patch over my eyes. They were light brown and didn't call much attention to themselves. They were happy. I was happy. It was when I discovered waxing one's eyebrows that things got out of hand.

Barbara A. Whittington

I watched the beauty operator wax patrons a few times. I was convinced I could follow suit. I bought a large container of eyebrow wax. A dab here and a dab there of hot wax and presto. Pull those hot patches off and I'd have beautiful eyebrows like every one else in that little shop. HELLO! Result: eyebrows crooked and eyelids raw and red.

About that time the beauty industry came out with an eyebrow razor. It was meant to serve those who had a steady hand and a healthy set of eyebrows. I did not possess either. Sure, the pink razor was tiny, but, oh, the damage it could do. I hadn't counted on blood either. Blood. For the first time in my eyebrow career. I had sores and blisters. Blood should not appear anywhere near one's eyes.

Tossing the razors, and eyebrow wax into the trash, I went back to having my eyebrows done by a professional. However, I'm still not without eyebrow dilemmas. Should one color one's eyebrows? Yes or no? Does one color brows the shade of her beauty shop tinted hair? Do you leave them the wide mixture that they have become with age? Salt, pepper, brown, yellow, or should one use the aged eyebrow pencil in the make up bag that is closer to auburn than light brown? Color them black as my sister did, or purple like the girl next door? The other option is to get rid of them permanently and paint on perfect ones.

Recently, I was told there is yet another option. Tattoo them on and they last forever, ending the dilemma of tweezing, razoring, coloring.

Nope. I swore when my husband came home from Hong Kong with a slightly indecent tattoo on his leg I would never go the tattoo route. For any reason.

I cannot speak to the trend of threading one's eyebrows, though I've seen girls at the mall threading brows with a thread so thin it's barely visible. Sharp as a razor too, as it slices through thick brows. Not an object I need in my hands.

I'm leaving the eyebrow issue for now. Today, I have a more pressing issue. A white hair sprouted out of my chin overnight.

Hair Dilemma

Lately I've lost my focus - again - on things I should be focusing on. I'm busy focusing on, well, here goes. My focus is entirely on a spot on my head. Yep, where I'm losing hair. I have one small spot on the right side of my head, in the exact position where my head hits the pillow every night.

I can't get my focus off that spot. Wondering why I have it, how I got it, what to do about it? Asking myself, will it get worse? Am I doomed to lose all my hair at this young age? Well, not so young, but who wants to have a bald spot at any age?

So instead of doing more important work, like painting my toenails, I'm trying to come up with remedies for my bald spot. Sure I can still cover it with hair, but who wants to look like those old guys who do comb-overs. I'm grateful the spot is not entirely bald. I now spend time in shops staring at hair products. My latest acquisition is a shampoo for thinning hair. I really don't know if it's helping but my hair smells like strawberries.

When Ray and I go shopping, I ask him repeatedly if my spot is covered. I drive him nuts checking the right side of my head. He always says yes, it's great, but can you trust a man who has already lost most of his hair, and sees his wife as the young girl he married, that girl who had loads of hair.

I'm slowly driving myself wild over this hair issue. I've tried sleeping in other positions to avoid the spot, but no matter what position I fall asleep in, I'm back on that spot when I wake in the morning, no doubt having ground the heck out of it all night.

I wear a mouth guard to keep from grinding my teeth at night. Is there such a thing as a head guard to protect my spot of thinning hair?

My mother wore a silk sleep cap to keep her hair in place. My husband thinks a sleep cap is the answer.

The real answer, though, is for me to stop grinding my head at night, but how?

I decided to color my hair, a semi permanent rinse. It makes one's hair thicker. The color was a brown shade. It went on jet black. Best not to have one's spouse home when one is coloring hair. After I passed him in the hall with black hair, he choked and said, "What the heck?" I could see he wasn't a fan.

When I washed the color off, my hair was dark auburn, a color I've never had. However, it's different and the bald spot is less noticeable. The color has made my hair fluffier. "Not fluffier," Ray said, grumpily. What does he know? I tossed my head. It was indeed fluffier.

Now, I intend to get my mind off my thinning hair and move on to something more pressing. Like the second hair growing out of my chin

Oh, I Love a Trip

We're getting ready for a change of scenery. We're heading to Wisconsin from our home in Ohio to visit our daughter and her family. The triplets will turn ten while we are there, and their little brother just turned six. We're so excited. I've been packing our bags and tucking in treats and little surprises all week.

We visited the Apple Barn and bought fresh apple butter, honey, and apples to take to them. You'd think we were taking a trip to Europe, the way we've been assembling items. Don't forget to take this or that, we keep reminding each other. Of course at our age, it's DO NOT forget to pack your medication. We'll only be gone a week but you'd think we were going for the winter. We both look forward to the trip. Especially with fall here and the leaves putting on a colorful show. Our trip will take us through Indiana and Illinois and then into Wisconsin. Any time we've traveled this route in the fall, we've been given a rare and welcome show by the beautiful landscape.

When we arrive the kiddies are beside themselves with joy and throw themselves into our arms. Of course we love and welcome every affectionate gesture. We haven't seen them for a few months and pictures tell us they've grown several inches.

They'll be surprised because Nana and Papa have a new car. They were used to riding around with us in the old gray sedan when they came to visit us. Now, one of the first orders of business will be to take them for a ride in the new vehicle. This one has shiny new buttons and switches and they'll try them all to Papa's delight. The windshield will be washed several times and the seats and mirrors adjusted.

I don't remember having these kinds of visits with my own grandmother. The only grandparent living when I came along was Grandma Casto and she was elderly. She wore her gray hair braided and wound around her head. Later in her life she kept it cut and permed. She got a perm every three months like clockwork. We always took her peppermint sticks when we went to visit. She let us play with the buttons in her button jar. She liked to stay home and went only to church. Will I turn into Grandma Casto? I might. However, I think it's unlikely.

Today, grandparents are more active perhaps because we're healthier and have more energy, or because we didn't live through the depression or work physically as hard as the generation before us.

Whatever the reason, I can't wait to climb into the car tomorrow and head off to Wisconsin where our youngest grandchildren are waiting for us with generous hugs.

What more could one ask in this life than to be loved by a child?

We've been blessed eight times with grand-babies and are thankful for each one.

Today, hug someone, if not a child, find a loved one and give him or her a hug.

Chase, Tanner, Mackenzie

Sad Good Byes

The visit to Wisconsin went by quickly. We were able to spend some special time with our daughter when the family was out of the house. We took her to lunch and she and I shopped. I came home with a nativity set, two pairs of jeans, a top, and a sweater.

Jackson, their French Bulldog, and Samson, their English Bulldog were excited to see us too. We enjoyed both dogs for all their individual traits. Jackson guards food. It doesn't matter who has the food. He stands on guard until every morsel is gone, I'm assuming to make sure he gets a crumb if it drops. He chases Samson away from the food area, and just looking at chunky Samson brings a smile to our faces.

While R hung around the house I went to three, fourth grade classes on Friday afternoon to be a mystery reader. I'm not sure the triplets were all that surprised that I showed up because they'd asked me beforehand, but they didn't know the day or time I'd appear. I read a randomly picked book from the nearby library called The Witchy Broom. I picked it because it was short and ended with a bit of suspense. My daughter took several photos of me in their classrooms. That day was the highlight of the trip for me, mostly because I had the opportunity to be with the grandchildren, to meet their teachers, and to encourage all the children to read. I mentioned that I write and urged them to try their hand at writing. That evening we had pizza and cupcakes for their birthday, and gave them their gifts. Books, of course. Books are food for the soul and they were a big hit. The weather was beautiful for our entire visit.

One day, I made a pot of Thai Chicken Soup with fresh cilantro and coconut milk. I picked up only two fans of the soup. Our daughter and her husband. My husband said it was okay and the kiddies said no thanks and ate Chinese left from the night before. My daughter and I loved the soup and polished off the last bowl.

Our home-going was sad. Some tears, many hugs. I just knew it was time to leave after six days. We were tired and they were too. We've learned it's best to leave while everyone is still happy.

However, I always leave a part of myself with them and I bring home a part of them with me. A few months back, Mackenzie gave me a half of a heart on a chain and she kept the other half for herself. It reminds us that we are in each other's hearts, she said.

Grandchildren are a precious commodity. Not one you can give away or trade, but one that touches your soul and stays in your heart.

Tanner and Nana with the book The Witchy Broom

The Good Life

One winter several years ago, my husband and I traveled to the Gulf Coast of Florida to visit my sister in a community built on a golf course.

At the core of the development is a beautiful community center with something for everyone, from painting and writing to golf and swimming.

We fell in love with the good life.

The good life floated in our heads as we drove through an ice storm on the way home.

A few weeks of cold slush later, we were saying, "Let's move to Florida."

We called a real-estate agent. By dark, a for-sale sign graced our yard.

The house would take months to sell, we said. We'd have plenty of time to think through the process.

The first couple to walk through the house bought it, giving us 30 days to vacate.

The next week we bought a house in the Florida golf course community with a yard enclosed by swaying palms and flowering hibiscus. We bought a golf cart and rode through the neighborhood congratulating ourselves on our fabulous new life.

Back in Ohio, we threw away, gave away and sold.

Soon we had the stuff of 30 years down to an amount that fit into a 50-foot truck, which our son-in-law drove to Florida.

The house in Ohio had been meticulously kept, with the amenities new and updated. The five-year-old house down south was downright needy.

While my husband hired workers to replace floors, strip wallpaper, paint walls, install new counter tops and rebuild our dream home, I had time to think about our children and grandchildren, 900 miles away.

Knowing that the airport was nearby provided little comfort.

I've done my share of air travel, but I'm beginning to adopt the attitude of my stepfather who said, "If God had meant us to fly, he would have given us wings."

As the weeks passed, I visited the dream house.

Men carried jackhammers and whistled while they worked on the stone patio; others hoisted ladders to blow insulation into the attic.

By then it was June and HOT as Hades.

I knew I'd be riding in a box soon and using up my air time quickly if I didn't call a halt to the good life. I begged to go home. Forget the new furniture ordered and the boxes stored in the garage. I wanted to go for a break, a reprieve. A trip to see my grand babies. Perhaps a quick trip to our doctor for some feel good pills. I was going to have to be drugged if I was to enjoy the good life.

After seeing the children and being able to breath again without anxiety attacks, I decided I couldn't live in the dream house in the fantasy world I'd created in my head. I wanted to be back in drought-ridden dreary Ohio. Where often ice storms in the winter keep us housebound. Where tornadoes sometimes touch down dangerously close, where on any given day I can see my children and grandchildren.

After a month we went back south. We packed the few things we'd unpacked, rented a truck, called our son-in-law to fly down and drive the truck home. Ah, home!

By then the house in Florida was truly a dream home. We sold it to a couple from Indiana who were in search of the good life. I hope they found what they were looking for.

As for me, I'm content being in another house on a little piece of land back in Ohio.

All this was several years ago but I often think back on the experience and realize I gained more than I lost. We live near one daughter, another lives not far away and while the youngest is eight hours away by car, I can still get to her in a day when I am longing to see her and her family.

Sometimes without even looking for it, the good life finds us.

"A good life is when you smile often, dream big, laugh a lot, and realize how blessed you are for what you have." Anonymous

City Litter versus Country Litter

Our home in the country has helped us redefine litter, a home in the country, you say. Fresh air. Green meadows. Bird watching. Oh, bliss.

Well, not so fast. Sure, you get all of that, plus you get a whole lot more! You get country litter.

We've lived in several places, enough to know there's a difference between city litter and country litter.

Our first home was a sixties ranch in a Cleveland suburb. Back then metal containers were placed along all roadways and trash became litter.

Still, there was the occasional wad of gum, candy wrapper, or paper cup tossed out.

Then, we moved to a custom ranch in an upscale neighborhood. Everything matched, from the mailbox to the shed in the backyard. It was the decade of stone and earth tones. There was little litter. If it existed it was in receptacles of stone or earth tones at the curb.

As retirees, we moved to the sunshine state. Thanks to moving on a sweltering June day, we stayed only long enough to pay the mover and set up a date for the return trip. The litter there came as boxes of fresh oranges and grapefruits left on curbs for those without fruit trees.

Back in Ohio, we tried apartment living. Daily trash pick up and a guy with a nail on a stick kept us litter free.

Next, we moved to a condo community where litter simply did not exist. There, ceramic geese in dresses abounded.

With a speed limit at 14 mph, if anyone had thrown out a popsicle stick, the condo cops would have caught it before it hit the pavement. Then they would have dragged the poor culprit to the clubhouse for bridge.

Now, we've moved to the country where we've learned the meaning of country litter.

There's a huge invisible sign on our front lawn that reads PLEASE DROP LITTER HERE. That means ALL your litter. Toss that drink carton our way and along with those 24 empties. That old ripped cushion, whiz it through the air into our driveway. Don't forget that banana peel.

Another thing we learned: it takes exactly ten miles driving time to inhale a million calorie lunch from McDonald's in town and make it to our place in the country. Quick. Duck. There comes the McDonald's bag with the remains of three BIG MACS, jumbo fries, two pies, a triple size chocolate shake, and a biggie soft drink.

Paper products are not all that is tossed. One can become the recipient of a mother beagle and six newborn pups overnight. By dusk we once possessed a hunting dog, a mother cat and seven kittens.

"Watch out." An item of clothing sails through the air. "Look. It's a hat." Okay, so, it blew off his head. That's understandable, however, his shirt too?

At least we don't have the invisible sign that fronts our neighbor's property down the road. DROP ALL APPLIANCES HERE. He recently woke to a lawn full of appliances in shades of avocado and gold.

Well, we're done moving. We're too old.

My only consolation is this country litter gives two old people something to do. There's much to discuss and to clean up.

I discuss. My husband cleans up.

My Sister Donna Sue

A few years ago, I made a trip to Tampa to visit my sister, Donna Sue, who was quite ill and in the hospital. We were able to have five days together. While I knew she was gravely ill, we shared many light moments where we were just big sister and little, hugging and giving each other advice. She wanted to take me shopping. "To buy you something," she said from her hospital bed. "We'll go to Beall's. They have such pretty things."

My sister had perfected the art of shopping. She could tell you which was the best mattress. What household appliance would outlast all others and mostly she could tell you where the best clothes for women could be bought. She didn't stint when it came to clothes. She bought the best. When she found slacks she liked she bought a pair in every color.

I borrowed a beaded white cardigan one day to wear to the hospital over a thin shirt because I often got chilled. When I entered her room she admired the sweater and said I believe I have one just like it. "This one is yours," I said. "You take it home," she offered.

"No! You might need it," I said, but she insisted. So I'm wearing it this week in her honor to keep off the chill of the rainy Ohio day as I read her obituary.

Barbara A. Whittington

She was and will always be my big sister. She watched me while mother worked when I was ages six to eleven. She looked out for me, shared her clothes, entertained me for hours on end.

Our step dad was gone, working shift work in a local plant.

I'll miss my sister for many reasons but the one most outstanding is that I'm not sure anyone will ever love me as much as she did. In her eyes, I was perfect. If we have even one such person in our lives, we are truly blessed.

I wrote this silly poem one year for Sue's birthday.

Oh, Donna Dear, your Birthday's here,
Whatever shall I do? Dance without shoes?
Sing you the blues? Oh, but ugh, those reviews!
You're near to my heart, sister, you gave me my start.
So here's a poem-present and I hope your day's pleasant.
I'll start with, "I love you. But, will that do,
For a sister who loaned me her white buck shoes,
And her very last bottle of Halo Shampoo?"
You danced and twirled and my straight hair curled.
A black-eyed beauty, you took serious this sister-duty,
While I spent my days in a summer haze
You walked us through that sister-maze.
Can you remember the smell of that sweet clover?
"Red Rover, Red Rover, Send my sister, Donna Sue, over!"
Oh, to spend one more day of my youth with you.
We'd even invite cousins, Anna and Sue.
For old times sake, fudge and popcorn we'd make.
And, to the Boogie Man an iron skillet I'd take!
Maybe we'll never make it to the moon,
But can you come over real ... uh...how do you spell SOON?
In memory of our letter-writing days,
And all my frustrating ways,
I love you still.
I always will.
Your Little Sister, Bobbie Ann

The day Sue died my husband was in the backyard. I went to tell him the news. Though it was expected it was a shock. Before I had a chance to say anything, he said, "I just saw Sue." He pointed to the sky. "There," he said, "she was dancing among those clouds."

We both firmly believe she was on her way to Heaven. Ray was not a person who "saw" things out of the ordinary and this was a first.

Sue loved the hymn Dancing Shoes by Squire Parsons. Sue's feet were crippled from rheumatoid arthritis and it was painful for her to walk. I believe she's dancing all over Heaven in her dancing shoes or even bare foot like we did in Hometown so long ago. Completely healed. Just like the woman in the Dancing Shoes song.

Me and Sue, the big sister who always looked out for the both of us.

Sue, Me, and Ella. Ella stayed home with us **after daddy died** while mother worked.

Loving Paul

I was four years old when I met Paul Warren. He was holding my sister Ella's hand. She and Paul were a match made in Heaven. I did not make a good impression on my sister's date. I didn't wear bright red lipstick or twirly skirts like Ella. Mostly I threw tantrums. I'd never been on "a date," and I wanted badly to go on one, particularly when I heard the date would involve beautiful girls in sequined costumes ice skating at a show called Holiday on Ice in Charleston. They were not happy when they caught me spying on them through the keyhole in the living room door that had been firmly shut. Ella stood on a footstool and was kissing tall Paul when I fell into the room.

He was the tallest man I'd ever seen and the most handsome, with his black curly hair. His friends even called him Curly. He drove a cab in Nitro and Pt. Pleasant before making his career in the Air Force.

When Ella and Paul married they became book ends, holding each other up and the good life they built between them. Oh, he might have been a step behind Ella all their lives but he never faltered. When Dawn came along I've never seen prouder parents. I didn't know Dawn had legs until she was two because her dad never put her down. When their beautiful son came along he had to put Dawn down because he had to chase Mark, his busy wonderful little boy. He did it with a smile. ALWAYS. His family was complete AND life was good. They lived in London, Japan, Okinawa, Louisiana, Florida, and finally Ohio.

Ella energized Paul's slow methodic ways. He softened her edges. Yes, the girls in my family have an edge!

Paul walked slower than the rest of us observing what we missed. He smelled the roses, the ones we walked passed or stepped on.

In his last years, Paul's destination and purpose has been to walk closer to the Lord.

I saw him change and grow. He was always tall among men but now he is taller than the highest cloud.

Most of us will never come close to where Paul was in his walk with the Lord, but we can always get on that path. He trod slower than the rest of us but he stayed the course until the day he went home to Heaven. Paul's never really been my brother in law. He's always been my brother. Rest in peace dear brother.

My husband and I went to visit Paul a few days before his death. When I approached the recliner where he sat, he said, "Bobbie, honey, you're standing in front of the Angels."

"Oh," I said, "I'll move," and I did. Quickly. I didn't want to hamper any angel activity. A few days later, Paul died. I believe he was accompanied home by those very angels that were in that room. I'm proud I knew Paul. I read the below prayer at at his funeral. It's called the Peace Prayer.

> The Prayer of St. Francis of Assisi
> Lord, make me an instrument of your peace
> Where there is hatred, let me sow love
> Where there is injury, pardon
> Where there is doubt, faith
> Where there is despair, hope
> Where there is darkness, light
> Where there is sadness, joy
> O divine Master, grant that I may not so much seek

A Girl from Hometown

To be consoled as to console
To be understood as to understand
To be loved as to love
For it is in giving that we receive
It is in pardoning that we are pardoned
And
It is in dying that we are born to eternal life.

Me, Paul, Sue

Ella and Paul's wedding photo

Good Bye to Summer

The weather is cooperating and we've been able to get outside and put away all the things we enjoyed during the summer weather in preparation for the season change.

We threw out the bedraggled red begonias from the front porch and all the dried geraniums from the back deck.

Our winters are often harsh so I'll clean and store our white wooden rockers in the basement. A gift from our daughter, Lisa. I love sitting in that rocker on the front porch when the weather is warm.

R has already stored our red metal chairs and table from the deck in his barn as well and the bigger table and chairs where we often have lunch - when I can get him off the lawn tractor!

I find comfort in putting to bed the items that bring me such joy in summer. I feel as though I'm wrapping them in a warm quilt to rest until beautiful weather when they'll claim their rightful place outdoors.

I put away the wooden green child's chair with the wreath and flowers. Even the pumpkins on the front step had to go yesterday as they were frozen and starting to rot! Is it that cold already?

Our fall leaves are at mid point in their descent. We have a few more to enjoy before the landscape turns barren and the trees will be dressed in ice crystals and glistening snow.

Other than a wreath on the front door covered in fall leaves, we'll be without decorations for a few weeks until it's time to bring out the sled for the front porch decked out with pine and red bows.

Outside my door the world will be yawning, preparing for a long nap. On the inside, I'll fill the house with pumpkin and cinnamon scent, soothing music, and be warm and cozy in a snuggie as I work to do some winter creating. I'll write, read, and dream of warm sunshiny days when I'll sit in the white rocker on the front porch and count the Cardinals in the front yard. Ray will probably be watching the Bluebird family return to their house in the side yard tree.

I'm thankful for each season that Our Creator has generously provided.

Each one offers its own individual beauty. For now, I'm in a holding pattern and looking forward to the brisk days when our thoughts turn to the holidays and to getting together with family.

Journey To The Creek Bed
with Granddaughters

Through tangled brush
We make our way
To the creek bed
Cooling summer feet
In crystal water.
Butterflies
With gossamer wings
Skitter up the bank,
Fanning honeysuckle vines.
Suddenly, a head shoots
From beneath a mossy rock,
A crawdad staking claim to his territory -
As if little girls pose a threat.
Later, on a picnic cloth
They arrange their treasures,
A speckled feather, an odd shaped
Rock, a golden leaf.
Unlike their "find," my treasures
Are images of two giggling girls
Arms outstretched
Ready to Embrace the world -
Ready to walk on water.

For Samantha and Jillian

Samantha and Jillian, a few years after our creek journey.

In My Mind I'm Always Going Home

Recently we went back to the old home-place on Cross Creek. Back to the farm in Buffalo, West Virginia where generations of Whittington's have been raised for over 100 years, the family farm that my husband's father inherited from his father.

The oil painting on our living room wall depicts the two-story farmhouse, the barn, and its outbuildings. It looks nearly the same today nestled there, a hillside farm in a cozy valley in Putnam County with cows roaming the pastures above.

Aunt Betty lives on the property adjoining the farm. The day we went to visit she stood in the doorway in her frilly white apron waving as our car pulled in her driveway. She looked for a moment like my mother-in-law who on many long-ago visits ushered us into the farmhouse kitchen where she had Sunday supper simmering on the stove.

Leafing through family albums, we saw dozens of baby ancestors. Babies now grown old. Deceased. Hiding both femininity and masculinity behind those long white dresses trimmed with lace.

We looked at beautifully painted plates found in the farmhouse attic and reminisced about the time our youngest got her head stuck in the railing leading to Aunt Betty's basement, causing much consternation as the adult tried to figure out a way to get the child's head dislodged, intact, and after much maneuvering, Aunt Betty came through. To everyone's delight. Particularly the child's.

We also remembered the time Aunt Betty had given this child hammer and nails and let her help build the gazebo that still stands in the backyard near where deer come daily to graze.

Funny how time changes things, even memories.

My husband remembers when mail was delivered on horseback. When there was no electricity on the farm. What it was like without television. To conserve water. To read by lamplight. To make do. Make do. Now there's a phrase few of us know.

His sister remembers the two of them sitting on a little wooden stool by the roadside next to the mailbox waiting to flag down a neighbor who would gladly take their nickel and bring back a banana popsicle from Hulbert's Store in Buffalo on hot summer days. My husband doesn't have this memory though Betty says she can still see him, his curly head resting in his hands, elbows on his knees, when it was his turn to sit on the stool. Back then no more than two or three cars passed by in a day's time. Now new homes springing up in the area have brought with them 24 hour traffic.

Yet as I looked down the hill at the farmhouse to the home where I came as a young bride, seeing the cows grazing in the sunny pastures, it was as though time had stood still, and I was transported back. To the porch where fresh canned vegetables stood cooling on the white enameled table, awaiting transport to their winter home in the cellar below. To the barn where fresh hay had been tossed down. To where a baby kitten was having its warm milk, fresh from the cow, in a pink and white saucer from the kitchen. Where the biggest thing we had to worry about was if there were enough chairs when we sat down to Sunday supper around the kitchen table laid with a scattering of rose-patterned Limoges and new white oil cloth. Where the scent of fried chicken and buttery mashed potatoes filled the air.

Then I looked beyond the hill. I saw the new houses. Heard the traffic coming around the bend in the road and realized it would soon be impossible to go back. Except in my mind. In my mind, I'm always going home.

The Whittington farm on Cross Creek

Betty and me

Grandchildren - Steven, Daniel, Jillian and Samantha at Aunt Betty's and Uncle Paul's farm.

BONUS CHAPTERS

MISSING: SWEET BABY JAMES

Chapter One

"Doreen Moon, if you don't hold still, I'm gonna hog-tie you to this chair!" Vada Faith whipped the pink salon chair around so she and Doreen were face to face. She shook her comb under Doreen's nose and the woman's eyes grew wide as china plates. "I'm a nervous wreck!" Vada Faith let out a long labored breath. "I've had six hair cuts since Joy Ruth left to take Mama to her doctor's appointment."

"Well, forgive me for living!" Doreen closed her tabloid ruffling the pages loudly.

"This day's been a disaster." Vada Faith swallowed hard, took a big breath, and blew her blond bangs off her forehead. "I'm sorry, Dorrie. The girls needed panty hose this morning for a school project. I had to wake up the baby and take him with us to the store." She smiled when she thought of James, who always woke up happy. "Then," she added, "I learned from a note in their book bag the girls had volunteered me to make pancakes this Friday, of all days! Fridays are crazy here!"

Vada Faith turned Doreen around so the woman could see herself in the mirror and started sectioning off her hair. "Their teacher, Miss Jenny, bought maple syrup at the farm they visited. Thus, the pancakes." She frowned at Doreen. "I dared them to volunteer me for anything else!" She shook her comb at Doreen's face in the mirror. "I'm done with that school."

"Calm down, honey." Doreen reached up and patted the beautician's arm.

Vada Faith breathed deeply as she wrapped another piece of gray hair around a roller.

"I'm sorry I can't sit still, honey." Doreen held up the tabloid. "It's this story. Someone has spotted an alien down on Bourbon Street. I hope it's moved on by the time they have that Mardi Gras in February. Imagine! An alien in the middle of that mess. Whew."

"That story isn't true, Doreen." Vada Faith glanced down at the tabloid. "Yep, that's the one. They make up stories and print them."

"This is The Very Latest News." Doreen shook the magazine. "Aliens is everywhere. I saw it on TV." She shook her head. "Oops, I moved again, sorry. I hope your mama's tests are good. I heard over at the coffee shop that Helena had a doctor's appointment."

Vada Faith put in the last roller and settled Doreen under a pink dryer.

Thankfully, Doreen would soon be combed out and gone. The woman had the most stubborn gray hair and she never stopped talking. Vada Faith grabbed the broom and swept up the hair around her chair.

"When you see your mama," Doreen called, popping her head out from under the dryer, "tell her I'll put her on the prayer list over at the New Believer Baptist Church. It's where I go now." She opened the tabloid. "I switched my membership from Heavenly Tabernacle when they got rid of Brother Bo Shannon. They said he was a big flirt." Doreen grinned, and said above the roar of the dryer, "Well, he was not! He was real friendly is all. Besides too many young Democrats go there now. You know those liberals. Always wanting to change things up." She sighed. "Don't forget to tell your mama about the prayers." The woman's words trailed off as she pushed herself back under the dryer.

Vada Faith nodded. She wondered how someone over at the coffee shop knew her mama had a doctor's appointment. Shady Creek was a cauldron of gossip.

Just then Cindy Mahan, her baby sitter, pushed through the shop door pulling eight-month old James behind in his stroller.

"Well, look who's here." Vada Faith smiled and went to help Cindy guide the stroller inside. Her beautiful baby smiled at her. His little hands gripped the front of the stroller and his eyes sparkled.

"We got bored," Cindy said, plopping into the nearest pink chair. "Me and Sweet Baby James. We couldn't find a thing to do. He got tired of peek-a-boo and his ABC blocks. We thought we'd come and visit. Didn't we, James?" She ruffled his blond hair. James smiled up at her and batted his big blue eyes. He was a little flirt already.

He clapped his hands and drooled on himself. He leaned over the stroller and stared at his new blue tennis shoes. He wore his blue shirt with the yellow bulldozer that read, "Daddy's Little Man."

"Check out this little guy's new Levi's." Vada Faith patted the baby's leg. "They fit him perfectly."

"I know." Cindy leaned over and hugged James. "Little Fashion King of Shady Creek. Oh," she added, "James has an admirer. An old woman in front of the diner. She leaned down and patted him on the foot. He kicked and squealed. The more he squealed, the more she laughed. He reached out and grabbed the fringe of her ugly brown shawl. Ugh! She called him Robert twice. I gave her his correct name. She shook her head and grumbled. Then she took off down the street."

"Well, buddy, are you collecting girlfriends?" Vada Faith watched as James chewed on his fingers and clung to his brown bear. He hugged the bear, giving her a toothy smile. He put his hands over his eyes.

"Peek a boo!" His mother covered her eyes.

James squealed and kicked his feet. One of his little blue shoes fell to the floor.

Vada Faith's heart swelled. She leaned over, put on his shoe and tied the lace. She picked up the baby and squeezed him. He jabbered over her shoulder and pointed at the lights.

She carried him to the magazine rack on the wall and held up the new Highlights magazine with children on the cover. He chewed his fingers and kicked his legs. He was cutting more teeth.

Doreen waved at the baby and Vada Faith took him to see her. "Hey, little fellow," she said, pulling herself out from under the dryer to pat him on the arm. "He's a doll, Vada Faith."

"Thanks."

James yawned as Vada Faith showed him around the rest of the shop. She put him back into his stroller and he promptly snuggled with his bear. "Time to go home, big boy." She kissed his cheek and smoothed down his blond hair. "Don't forget, Cindy, I'll be home early today."

Cindy nodded and buckled James into his seat. Vada Faith helped her get the stroller out onto the sidewalk and nodded as they turned to go toward home.

She waved them off and went to pour a cup of coffee. There was a lull in the shop so she picked up a magazine and leafed through it, thankful for the quiet.

When Doreen's dryer stopped, Vada Faith styled her hair and hugged her on her way out the door. Relieved the shop was finally empty, she drank from her bottle of water on the counter and added some items to her grocery list. She enjoyed going home early to be with James.

"Mama's feeling fine," Joy Ruth said, coming in the door. "She had blood work, a chest x-ray, and a mammogram." She slung her purse on the counter by her station. "Anyway, she'll have the results in a few days. I think she's just been tired. I'm doing her hair this afternoon."

"Great." Vada Faith grabbed her purse. "She can't be very sick if she wants her hair done. Well, I'm out of here. I need to hit the grocery then home to my boy."

"Sure. I'll stop by on my way home to see him."

Vada Faith headed for the door, glad she'd be home soon. "See you later."

As she rushed out of the shop, she had no idea her world was about to change forever.

Chapter Two

The old woman straightened her brown shawl around her shoulders. Her big sister had made the shawl for her. The baby in the stroller had jerked on it pulling it lopsided. He recognized Birdie. She smiled and walked down the street. The baby in the carriage was Robert, her baby brother, even if the girl said no. Birdie shook her head, trying to clear her thoughts. Where did the girl go in such a hurry? Why did she have Robert and take him away from her, his sister?

Her mind scrambled things like a mixer in a bowl of eggs. Like the directions to Sissy's house. Her mind had held the directions firmly in place until the minute she needed them. Then, poof, they disappeared, flying away to an inaccessible place in Birdie's head. Sissy instructed her to always ride the bus to her house. The swaying of the bus had lulled Birdie's tired body into a peaceful sleep. The directions to Sissy's house had taken flight.

Sissy reviewed the directions with Birdie each time she came to her house. However, this was a surprise visit. Birdie had left the home for crazy people in the middle of the night, with the key she'd stolen. There'd been no review of landmarks.

When the bus jostled to a stop and the driver called, "Shady Creek," Birdie woke with a start. Not knowing what to do, she disembarked with the other passengers. The streets went in every direction, baffling Birdie.

Her sister's warning rang in her ears. "Don't talk to anyone." So, she clamped her mouth shut for fear she might blurt out she was lost.

Scared, Birdie made her way past the Main Street sign with tears streaming down her cheeks and headed into a neighborhood lined with houses.

Chapter Three

After an early lunch, Vada Faith leaned back in the front porch swing and pushed off with her bare foot. She smiled over at James sitting in his playpen sorting through his toys. She had changed his clothes putting him into his soft blue pants and matching Peter Rabbit shirt and bib. That little guy was the best thing that had happened to her since the birth of her twin girls eight years earlier. It helped with the heartbreak of the miscarriage she'd had a few years back.

Today the street was unusually quiet for such a sunny fall day. She liked the convenience of living a few streets from the center of town. Their old Victorian home, once owned by her husband's grandmother, Belle Waddell, now belonged to her family. As the town grew it encompassed the big home. It stood regally among a row of pastel bungalows, the perfect place to raise a family.

Vada Faith opened a magazine looking for new hair styles. A few of her customers wanted something different every week.

Just then the kitchen buzzer sounded through the open living room window. She closed the magazine and let the swing glide to a stop.

"Hey, buddy," she said to James, who chewed on his yellow duck. Her heart swelled at the sight of him. She patted the baby on his blond head as he pulled up to the side of the pen. He smiled, showing off his four front teeth.

"Mommy loves you, too." She bent and kissed him on the cheek. He dropped to his bottom to investigate the snaps on his pants. He was such fun to watch. Earlier, he had tried to catch the shadows that fell over the teddy bear design of his play pen pad. He waved his arms in the air. When a butterfly landed on the play pen, he clapped his hands. "Mama," he said, looking straight at Vada Faith, his blue eyes crinkling in a grin.

He'd only said mama a time or two. Dada was what he said the most. She didn't mind. John's happiness when James said it was enough for her. He was a great dad.

As she opened the screen door to go inside, she turned and glanced back. She watched James roll onto his belly and start jabbering as a bug marched across the porch floor. A bottle of milk lay beside him.

She hummed as she took the apple pie from the oven and slipped it onto a mat on the counter. She turned off the oven. A meat loaf cooled beside the pie. The kitchen smelled wonderful. When she had pie later, James would have some fruit sauce his grandmother made for him. Her mother, Helena Warfield, possibly the world's worst mother, was this amazing grandmother. She even made baby food for James, including teething biscuits from her own recipe.

Vada Faith's relationship with her mother had been on solid ground since the birth of James. Helena had left Vada Faith and Joy Ruth, her twin sister, with their father when they were toddlers. Delbert Waddell could've used a few parenting classes. It hadn't been easy but now she and Joy Ruth were adults and life was good. With the arrival of James, Vada Faith became more tolerant and forgiving of her mother. There was something to be said for growing up. Maturing. Maybe it came with having a "last" baby. Squeals of delight wafted through the front window as James made some new discovery on the porch floor.

"Coming, James," she called toward the hallway leading to the porch.

"I-love-you," she sang, opening the refrigerator door as Barney's theme song rolled off her tongue. "You-love-me, we're-a-hap-py-fam-i-ly!" She grabbed a bottle of water for herself and a bottle of juice for James. She had to laugh as the jingle played over in her head. She'd sworn never to watch Barney again when the girls outgrew him. Now she was playing the dvd's for James and singing along as he clapped. She was happy as a mother bird clucking over her brood. That was how James made her feel. Happy. Content. Her life was perfect.

The phone rang, interrupting her thoughts. The church secretary at Sunnyside Baptist needed two dozen cupcakes for the youth meeting on Saturday. Vada Faith found a scrap of paper and jotted a note to herself, leaving it on the counter as a reminder to bake the cupcakes. Then she hurried back to the porch and her baby boy.

Chapter Four

"Here we go, Sweet Baby James." Pushing open the screen door with her toe, Vada Faith held the baby's juice bottle in mid air. The blinding sun made her blink a couple of times. She stumbled out the door, turning toward the play pen.

It was empty.

"James?" She shook her head to clear her vision. "James," she said. Then, she looked into the play pen and screamed, "Baby! James! Where are you?" She dropped the two bottles in a chair, and pushed aside the mound of toys in the pen. No baby boy.

"James!" She hurried across the front porch, looking in every corner.

"James!" She pulled her basket collection from under the long white church pew John had painted. Her son wasn't there. Her heart pounded.

She ran to the play pen. Where could he be? Could he have stood on the toys and climbed or fell out? She hadn't heard a cry. She'd heard only happy chatter. She dashed to the middle of the front yard.

"James!" Not one sound could be heard. Not even a dog barked.

She ran around the house, kicking through a pile of leaves the girls had left the day before.

Back on the front porch, she gripped the sides of the empty play pen. Where was he? How could he be gone? Her stomach knotted. Her breakfast threatened to come up. She walked to the sidewalk, her fists clenched at her sides. Had her mother picked up the baby? No. Her sister? Never. Joy Ruth was doing their mother's hair at the beauty shop.

Neither would take James without asking. They knew Vada Faith was paranoid about her children. She stared up and down the street.

Silence.

Suddenly, it came to her.

"Harriet," she screamed, tearing across the street towards Harriet Mitchell's yard. She prayed Harriet had James. The woman had taken him from his pen a few months back wanting to show him the birds at her feeder.

That day, Vada Faith hadn't heard Harriet step onto the porch. She'd been planting flowers along the side of the house. Thankfully, she heard James squealing as the woman carried him to the sidewalk.

Now, she paused to get her breath. A For Sale sign loomed in front of Harriet's house. How could she have forgotten? Harriet was in a nursing facility and had been for weeks. Was she losing her mind like Harriet?

"My baby, James!" Vada Faith gasped as the dispatcher answered her 911 call. "He's missing!" She stood in the kitchen gripping the cell phone.

"James?" the woman repeated. "Missing?"

"Yes, my baby boy, James! One minute he was on the front porch in his play pen." She paced the kitchen. "The next minute he was gone.

"Please," she pleaded, "someone has to find my baby. He's only eight months old. He was taken from my porch a minute ago. Vada Faith and John Waddell. The old Waddell place."

Tears ran down her face, dripping onto her new blouse. She had put it on with such care that morning while the baby crawled happily around her in circles. She wiped her tears with her free hand.

"Vada Faith Waddell! Oh, yes," the dispatcher responded, "Officer Cobb will be right there. Calling him now. He's at the gas station. You hang on, honey. He'll be there in a jiffy."

When Vada Faith put the phone down, she dropped into a kitchen chair, frozen with panic. She put her head on the table and wept.

Other books by Barbara A. Whittington -
Available at Amazon and Select book stores.

Vada Faith
Missing: Sweet Baby James
Ezra and Other Stories
Dear Anne: Love Letters from Nam

www.ingramcontent.com/pod-product-compliance
Lightning Source LLC
Chambersburg PA
CBHW051055160426
43193CB00010B/1190